The Harvard
Entrepreneurs
Society's Guide to
Making Money

The Harvard Entrepreneurs Society's Guide to Making Money Or The Tycoon's Handbook

By the founders of
the Harvard
Entrepreneurs Society
Edward A. Gazvoda, Jr.,
and William M. Haney III,
with John Greenya

Little, Brown and Company
Boston   Toronto

FIRST EDITION

Library of Congress Cataloging in Publication Data
Gazvoda, Edward A.
    The Harvard Entrepreneurs Society's guide to making money, or, The tycoon's handbook.

    1. New business enterprises. 2. Entrepreneur.
I. Haney, William M. II. Greenya, John. III. Harvard Entrepreneurs Society. IV. Title.
HD62.5.G39 1983   658.4'2   83-12075
ISBN 0-316-30590-1

The Harvard Entrepreneurs Society is a nonprofit undergraduate business society, organized by the authors of this book. The ideas, opinions, facts, and conclusions expressed in this book represent the authors' ideas, opinions, facts, and conclusions, and in no way imply approval or endorsement by Harvard University, or any of its faculties or administrators.

BP

Published simultaneously in Canada
by Little, Brown & Company (Canada) Limited

PRINTED IN THE UNITED STATES OF AMERICA

To our parents and their parents,
for their love and support

Contents

Acknowledgments

We wish to give a special thanks to John Greenya for his constant patience and creativity in helping us construct this book.

It is impossible to give adequate expression of our thanks to those without whom Fuel Tech and all the personal rewards associated with it would never have become a reality. Joe, Walter, James, Howie, Robin, Ger, Frank — without you, Fuel Tech would be like work. Thanks.

We also would like to take this opportunity to thank many of the people whose probing questions and thoughtful suggestions have provided us with the experience that our years could not. Special thanks to Brad Field, Helen Ver Standig, Barbara Everett, Bradford Mueller, Fredrick and Jacomina Nicholas, Paul Gruenberg, Daniel Delvecchio, and Professors Bales, Chandler, Markham, McClelland, and Stevenson.

Finally, we can only be grateful for the outstanding collection of ne'er-do-wells who allow us to call them our friends. The support of our peers, the genuine concern and incessant teasing, has allowed these ventures to remain amusing and enjoyable. Our friends cannot receive enough thanks. Mark, Bernie, Sean, George, RG, Paul, Michael, Eric, John, Face, Peter, Emmett, Gus, Ann, Jenny, Heather, Kendall, Leonie, RJ, Tyler, Rob, Mike, Ben, SoYun, Tony, PK, Mark, Mandy, Mehmet, Bob, George, Steve, Michelle, and Charlie, thank you.

Special affection to Anne and Lisa.

Introduction

To a degree, entrepreneurism is what one does in college now for excitement, a productive excitement. This is now the socially acceptable thing.

> — *Professor Howard H. Stevenson*
> *Graduate School of Business*
> *Administration, Harvard*
> *University*

That statement may surprise some people, especially those who went to college in the 1960s and 1970s, but it is true. We know it is true from our own experience.

In the 1960s, students turned to activism as their way of trying to deal with the issues of the day that mattered deeply to them. In the next decade, students' excess energy was often turned inward, a reflection of the so-called Me Generation. One of those interviewed in this book, law student John Kopchik, was a Harvard undergraduate in the mid-1970s, and he recalls, "There couldn't have been a Harvard Entrepreneurs club when I was a freshman here in 1976. It wouldn't have been 'cool.' "

There is definitely such a club on this campus today, and its ever-increasing popularity reflects the strong interest in entrepreneurial business activities on the part of college students — and people of all ages — throughout the country. Even a brief glance at the last few reports from the Harvard registrar's office shows that something is going on: in 1981–1982, the most popular academic major at Harvard was Economics (which is as close as you can come to majoring in business); five years ago, it was a near tie between Economics and Biology; and ten years ago, Economics was a distant sixth, trailing behind Government, English, Social Relations, History, and Biology.

This is not a local or a regional phenomenon. The same kind of booming interest in business among undergraduates can be seen in California (Stanford especially), the Midwest, and all through the South. College students are as worried as their elders about the economy and the problems besetting the country. Their response is to go out and make money; they are showing their faith in the free-enterprise system.

We never planned to write a book. We were too busy trying to combine school and business. But in December of 1981, a reporter for the *New York Times* wrote an article about undergraduate business activity at Harvard, and our experiences were featured. Our company, Fuel Tech, was mentioned prominently, and it was pointed out that we were the founders of the Harvard Entrepreneurs Society. That was the beginning.

One of the many calls and contacts that resulted from that article was from a publisher who wanted to hire us to interview our fellow student entrepreneurs on a flat-fee basis so that he could then put it all together as a book. That struck us as a very bad business deal, so we decided to do it ourselves (with a little professional help). This book is the result of that decision.

As you will learn from reading what follows, we have been involved in business ventures of all sizes and natures, from the small to the very large, from the simple to the extremely complex. We have worked with people of all ages and from all walks of life, and as a result we learned a lot of lessons.

The most important of all those lessons is that you have to have faith in yourself.

The first thing you don't need is a Harvard education, or any extensive formal education, to succeed in most businesses. What you *do* need is common sense, the ability to work hard, and a belief in yourself. Over and over again, we have run into people who have tried to put us down because we were "too young," "inexperienced," or "dreamers." We were finally able to see that the real problem was *theirs,* not ours, and since then we have done well.

The people you will meet in this book have also done well. That doesn't mean they have become rich, for in almost every case that was not their goal. They have done well because they have accomplished their objectives, small, medium, and large. Many of them, like us, didn't know how large those objectives were until they were well on the way to achieving them, but that is a large part of the lesson.

We will introduce you to approximately two dozen of our fellow undergraduate entrepreneurs, who will tell you how they started their business ventures and guide you through the pitfalls to expect and avoid. Recognizing that the needs and interests of all readers will not be the same, we've divided the various business ventures into three categories — "Small," "Medium," and "WOW!" Book One contains examples of several types of money-making ventures that are either one-time or seasonal and should appeal to readers whose time and funds may be limited; Book Two contains examples that are more ambitious, in a sense, but may still be easily duplicated by anyone who has the ability to work hard and enough desire; Book Three — "WOW!" — includes those ideas that have turned into large, full-time, and quite profitable businesses; none represents an impossible dream.

One common theme runs through the interviews: entrepreneurs do not like to work for other people, and when they do they like to have a lot of independence. If you find that you would much rather work long, odd hours for a chance at a bigger payoff than work a regular set of hours for the minimum wage (or face a lifetime of nine to five at the same job) then you are the person for whom this book is meant.

Another theme is that while they share certain characteristics, such as the one mentioned above, entrepreneurs come in all sizes and shapes and many different varieties. Do not be discouraged if your background or education or training is not exactly the same as that of the successful business types written about in such magazines as *Forbes* or *Business Week*. As long as you have faith in your own idea, and are willing to work hard at it, you are just as much of an entrepreneur.

Also, if you happen to be young, whether in school or not, you will run into people who dismiss you and your idea simply because you are not older and more experienced. We believe that being young should be an asset, not a liability. But it will be your job, as it was and still is ours, to convince people of that vital fact.

Finally, we believe very strongly that entrepreneurs and small businesses will play a very large role in the economic revitalization of this country. Is it an accident that so many young people are interested in business these days? We think that it signals a healthy impatience with the status quo, and, what's more, one that actually could "change the system from within." We welcome you to our ranks.

Ed Gazvoda, class of '83
Bill Haney, class of '84
Cambridge, Massachusetts
January 1983

BOOK ONE

Small or It's All a Matter of Perspective

1

"Hey, Buddy, Wanna Buy Some Firewood?"

At ten o'clock on a late fall morning in 1980, our dream materialized as an eighteen-wheel tractor-trailer carrying a huge load of firewood pulled into the Harvard Business School parking lot off Webster Avenue in Cambridge, Massachusetts. A cheer went up from the small group of undergraduate students as the truck came into view. As the huge diesel rumbled closer, the cheers turned into expressions of awe.

No one present, and certainly neither one of us, had ever seen so much wood, at least not horizontal. The truck contained thirteen cords of wood, which meant — with a single cord measuring four feet by four feet by eight feet — the load, if also piled at a height of four feet, would cover 416 square feet, or almost the entire parking lot. To put it another way, it was like seeing a football field covered with one and a half feet of wood.

Staring over that sea of wood, neither one of us had the heart to tell our crew of fellow classmates that the thirteen cords was not even the full order. Another truck, bearing twelve more cords, was on its way, and a third was scheduled to deliver the final seven cords later, directly to Harvard Yard.

After the truck had left, and the crew was busily loading as many cords of firewood as it could get into the
two rented U-Haul vans for transport to Harvard's
Freshman Yard, where our customers were waiting, we
looked at one another and grinned. Our first joint venture
was a very obvious reality. In a little over a week, the
"firewood deal" had gone from conception to potential
execution. All that we had to do was make delivery and
collect the rest of our money. The firm of Edward A.
Gazvoda, Jr., and William M. Haney III was open for
business. We stopped to grin at each other for a moment,
and then we hurriedly pulled on our gloves and began to
load wood.

The whole thing had started because a roommate of
Ed's had seen an ad in a local newspaper, while they
were sitting in a Laundromat one cold afternoon, and
said, just kidding around, "Hey, Ed, you're the schemer,
the guy who's always looking for ways to make money.
Why don't you sell firewood?"

Even though he knew the guy was kidding, Ed took
the idea seriously. He knew that there were a lot of
fireplaces at Harvard, and he also knew that the local
wood dealers got a real good price for it. That was the
beginning.

Ed started pricing wood, calling a couple of places in
Connecticut and Maine, checking all the local prices.
After that he did a little survey around the dorm, and
almost everyone he talked to said he wanted wood if he
could get it for less than the local prices. And the price
Ed was talking about was almost *half* — $26 for a quarter-
cord. Of course, we almost got arrested at first because
we thought we were selling *face cords* — each about an
eighth of a full cord of wood, using the standard measure.
But we got that straightened out.

While Ed was knocking on doors he met a guy who
was also planning to sell firewood, a junior named Meh-

met Oz, who turned out to be one of the best entrepreneurs on campus. He got all upset when Ed told him he had the whole campus sewed up already — which wasn't quite true but was the same story he told Bill Haney a few days later when he knocked on his door and met him — but he calmed down and eventually the three of us became partners, though in the end the two of us were the main partners.

Originally, we were concerned whether or not we would be able to sell twelve cords, the minimum huge truckload on which we could get a fantastic discount — seventy bucks a cord if we got to twelve cords. Our next goal was to get *two* of these trucks, which is where Bill came in. With him selling to the freshmen and Mehmet to the upperclassmen, and Ed selling to anyone he could find, we went *over* the twenty-four cords. We could hardly believe it.

Actually, Bill had almost been a competitor, rather than a partner. His dorm proctor had asked him if he wanted to sell some wood, because Bill had been one of the group who had organized all the first-week parties, gone around and collected all the money, and bought the kegs of beer. He'd met a *lot* of people that way. When approached by the proctor, he'd sort of said both yes and no to the wood deal; the idea had appealed to him, but he hadn't done anything about it when Ed came and knocked on his door, trying to sell him wood.

As it turned out, Ed was in kind of a touchy position because Bill's proctor wasn't exactly crazy about Ed — and Ed wasn't exactly crazy about him. When the proctor learned about Ed's visit, he warned Bill not to work with him. He told Bill that Ed was "off the wall." But, as it turned out, that's what appealed to Bill more than anything else.

Part of Ed's problem with Bill's proctor was that on his first day at Harvard Ed had gone to see this same guy and told him that he didn't care what courses he took that semester as long as they were the four easiest courses at Harvard — which was *not* a smart thing to do.

Despite the proctor's warning, Bill called Ed back the next day and told him he'd work with him. Ed said he was going to pay Bill $40 a cord out of the $100 or so he was charging. Later, he claimed he'd given Bill a better deal in order to "motivate" him!

With our combined attitudes and approaches, we really went crazy selling that wood. Almost every room bought some. For a while we were selling wood as an aphrodisiac, telling guys how much their girl friends would appreciate a nice fire. We were just pushing it out the door. Fortunately, it was still early in the school year, when students, especially freshmen, still have a lot of money, and they were buying it with sort of a "why not?" attitude. So, by the time the wood was set to arrive, we had done a whale of a selling job.

The day before the wood was to come, we went to the office that arranges university parking and told someone there we were working on a deal for one of the dorms, but that in order not to block any fire lanes we thought it would be best to have our wood dropped off at the B School parking lot. He agreed. Of course, we only said "some" wood, on the theory that the less you tell Harvard (or probably any school where you are a student) the better.

When the trucks arrived, the loads of wood were piled so high that when the back of the truck would go down to let the wood roll off, the front would rise up in the air two stories! We had a mountain of wood at first, and we leveled it and started loading it into the U-Hauls we had available, and then suddenly all these kids started arriving with anything they could think of for carrying wood — newspapers, bags, four strong friends. One guy even showed up with a baby carriage.

Some kids complained about having to carry the wood,

and a few even said they didn't like the quality of the wood, in which case we gave them their money back right away, no questions asked. But by day's end we had gotten rid of it all, and Ed was carrying a huge wad of cash — several thousand dollars, and that was after paying the truck drivers.

But it was not done without any number of problems. When the truck arrived to deliver the load inside Harvard Yard, it turned out that the Yard was closed for the first time since the 1960s because the Med School people were threatening to strike. All the gates were closed, and security guards and undercover agents were posted everywhere. And there we were trying to get a tractor-trailer full of wood into historic Harvard Yard. Both of us had key roles to play.

Bill was riding along with the guy who was driving the tractor-trailer and didn't know where in the world he was going. They pulled up in front of one of the locked gates, but as it turned out, Bill had a key to it! (How he got it is a different story.) At first he was going to open it himself and just say the hell with it and go in with the wood, but a security guard came along.

As it happened, Bill knew him. In fact, they had gone drinking together. So Bill suggested the guard call a certain dean (with whom he'd also gone drinking), which the guard did, and the dean said okay. In we went.

Now this truck was huge, and historic Harvard Yard is very fragile; everybody was *very* worried that we'd do some damage. Finally we got the wood dumped, right next to Lehman Hall, one of the dorms, and the pile was *incredible*.

Then the truck got all tangled up in a valuable old Harvard tree that had probably been in the Yard for several centuries. And then, of course, another dean came along and asked Bill what he thought he was doing.

By this time there was a huge audience, hundreds and hundreds of kids, and they were laughing and jeering and shouting at us to do something, probably hoping we'd end up with our asses in a sling. Suddenly, Ed scaled the truck! Up he went, several stories high, until he was standing on top of the upraised truckbed, trying to get the valuable branch loose before it snapped off. Suddenly, he did it, and the crowd went wild!

Finally, at about two in the morning, we were all finished. All the wood was sold and removed from the Yard. And the B School parking lot was all swept clean, a real Herculean task. The biggest human problem we'd had was with the students from the Law School. They were the only ones who kept calling and complaining, threatening to get us into trouble, to sue us, and all of that if we didn't get them their wood on time.

By three in the morning we had finished our pizza and hamburgers and beer and were counting out and dividing the money. The whole thing had taken nine days, from idea to execution, and in that time Ed had made $550, Bill $425, and Mehmet Oz almost $400. And we had really worked only a couple of days.

As a result of the wood deal, we decided to continue working together. We knew we could both work hard, and we had a feeling that our strengths and weaknesses were compatible. Where one of us wasn't strong, the other one was. And that was the start of our partnership. Two years later, we would be the founders and chief officers of a company that had capitalization of close to half a million dollars.

The moral of the story is that it pays to go to the Laundromat.

GAME PLAN To Sell Firewood

A. Market: Most Harvard students enjoy the luxury of a working fireplace in their dorm rooms. A market was already available.

1. Approach: The use of door-to-door salesmen provided a low-cost means for selling the wood. Also, using students as the "marketing arm" of the wood deal allowed the student consumers to identify with the product.
2. Price: The price was set at about half the market value. Selling in quantity was the key to a successful venture.
3. Timing: This venture had to be undertaken right before the advent of cold weather, and before competitors could saturate the market. As illustrated, other students had planned to capture the same market, but the expeditious (9 days) and expansive (all dorms) coverage of the market secured the success of this venture.

B. Competition: Other students who planned to sell wood and the established wood-delivery businesses.

C. Goods and Overhead
1. Materials: A source of wood at a low price was the key to this business. Gloves for handling the wood represent the only other material necessary.
2. Equipment: Getting the wood to Harvard was accomplished by subcontracting for delivery. A small transport truck was used for distributing the wood to the various dorms.
3. Facilities: The Harvard Business School parking lot provided the space necessary to handle the enormous loads of the two eighteen-wheelers full of wood.

D. Regulations: There are codes governing the transfer of wood in relation to measuring the volume of wood. Before a venture of this nature is undertaken, the local authorities should be consulted as to specific regulations governing the transfer of wood.

E. Capital: Several thousand dollars were needed up front to pay for the wood and delivery; additional money was needed to pay salespersons and workers.

Source: A deposit was collected by the salesperson on taking the order; this accounted for about one-third of the cash. Balance of the payment on each order was due on delivery; this accounted for the total income. To meet payments for the wood and delivery, it was necessary to borrow close to $1,000 from a friend — later named, appropriately, "loan shark" for the 2 percent interest rate he charged for *one day's* use of his funds. Payment for the second eighteen-wheeler delivery was met with money generated from the sale earlier that morning of the first two truckloads of wood.

F. Risk

1. Financial: This risk was minimal since the wood was durable and orders were secured before purchase. The markup on the wood was sufficient to absorb unseen costs.

2. Hidden Dangers: Conducting business on campus, especially door to door, is prohibited by the university with very few exceptions. The possibility of expulsion existed.

G. Time Commitment: This can easily be done part time for quick cash or full time, with no special talents or capital necessary.

H. What's Involved

1. Finding an inexpensive source of wood.
2. Determining the size of market.
3. Estimating market penetration.
4. Determining best means to reach that market.

5. Establishing means of distributing the wood.
6. Taking orders.
7. Delivery.

It's interesting that firewood, for centuries a real necessity, is now priced as if it were a luxury. But that makes it possible for an enterprising person to make good money selling it as either a one-time or an ongoing venture. However, as relatively easy as it sounds, there are certain essential precautions. One is to make certain not only of the *wholesale* price but also of the *quality* of the wood. If you end up with bad wood, after telling your customers they'd be getting top quality, you can forget about selling to them again.

Notice that not a great deal of capital is needed — if we could get over twenty cords of wood for an outlay of $1,500, then you can certainly get quite a bit of wood for quite a bit less money.

One of the reasons our wood deal worked as well as it did was that we didn't promise delivery to the customer's door. Be very careful if you contemplate doing that because it can increase your expenses enormously. (You'll find all sorts of customers who want the wood put in a special place, and that will take an inordinate amount of time.)

Finally, it wouldn't hurt to have a backup source of both wood and labor — just in case.

2

A Lot of
Little Deals

As the 1980s began, the academic choices of Harvard (and Radcliffe) students already indicated that a number of things had changed from previous decades. "Fields of Concentration of freshmen in Harvard and Radcliffe colleges" — or what most colleges used to call "majors" — provide an interesting picture.

The most popular field of concentration, as listed by the registrar's office on a computer printout dated May 8, 1981, was Economics. The total number of 170 (135 Harvard, 35 Radcliffe) represented 11.7 percent of the entire student enrollment. For the record, the study of Economics is the closest Harvard lets you come to a major in Business. In fact, the alphabetical order moves from "Biology" to "Chemistry" without so much as a double space.

In 1980–1981 the next most popular fields of concentration were:

Biology	7.8%
Government	7.4
History	6.6
Psychology and Social Relations	6.2
Biochemical Sciences	5.9
Social Studies	5.6

History and Literature	4.8
English and American Literature and Language	4.6
Engineering and Applied Science (A.B.)	3.5

One year later, Economics was still the most popular major, with 13.3 percent. Government attracted 8.1 percent and Biology 8.0 percent. The next most popular fields of concentration were History (6.9%), English and American Lit. (6.1%), Psychology and Social Relations (6.0%), and Biochemical Sciences (5.9%).

Five years ago, the picture was different. Economics and Biology were in a near tie for first place — 10.8 percent to 10.2 percent, respectively.

Five years before that, in 1971–1972, the picture was *very* different. That year's leaders were:

Government	12.6%
English	10.7
Social Relations	9.7
History	8.5
Biology	8.0
Economics	6.5

In ten years' time the number of Harvard students choosing to major in economics has more than doubled.

This is clearly not something that is happening only at our school or in our part of the country. Even before the article about us appeared in the *New York Times,* we'd been hearing about — and from — students on other campuses who were engaged in money-making ventures. There has been a program at Pittsburgh's Carnegie-Mellon for years, and Stanford, on the West Coast, has a very exciting history of encouraging entrepreneurial ventures. And we have heard of other programs operating everywhere from the Big Ten to the Deep South.

These are almost all *undergraduate* programs. The renewed interest in business is not something being imposed "from the top down" by professors of business administration encouraging experimental learning, but expressions of genuine interest that are bubbling up all across the country.

Thus our point in including these enrollment figures is that business and business-related studies are back on campus in a big way. To illustrate that interest, we have our own experiences and those of scores of our fellow students.

The remainder of this chapter will introduce you to a number of Harvard undergraduates who have been involved in small, and successful, entrepreneurial ventures.

The Crimson Christmas Tree Trekkers

Gerrit Nicholas is a twenty-year-old sophomore from Hartford, Connecticut. He has worked with us on a number of deals, including beer mugs (about which the less we say the better) and was in on the formation of Fuel Tech. Like so many of the kids who became members of the Harvard Entrepreneurs Society, Gerrit has an industrious (if not illustrious) past.

At the age of fourteen, Gerrit had his own "landscaping" company, which is to say, as he does, "I used my father's mower to cut all the lawns in the neighborhood." But he is being modest. After a short time, he realized there was an easier way than doing every lawn himself, so he hired two other kids from the neighborhood to cut the lawns. He paid them by the hour and got paid himself by the job. "I had other guys making money for me." Of course he did a lot of lawns all alone, but if he had wanted to, he could have rested and let his "business" pay him a profit. (We're kidding a bit, because anyone who is responsible for other workers has a whole new crop of headaches, such as dealing with the customers, keeping the equipment in running order, and scheduling; but the great majority of kids who have done it find they much prefer that type of work to pushing around a heavy mower in the hot sun.)

Once he got to Harvard, Gerrit Nicholas continued to work.

The first time I went into anything more "intriguing" than just little pickup jobs was when a bunch of us were sitting around and we were all broke, even though we all had been working for an agency on campus where anybody can get a job. But we were only making $3.50 an hour, and we just weren't getting very far.

Someone said, "Why don't we do something on our own to make money?" This was around November, so we thought, "What's coming up? Christmas." We set up Crimson Christmas Tree Trekkers, which was a business where we delivered Christmas trees to metropolitan Boston and other areas, such as Beacon Hill and Back Bay. One of our roommates lived in Back Bay and he said that although it's a rich area, a lot of people there don't have cars, and they have to lug their trees on the subway. Which is a definite drag. So we thought that might be a good idea.

We printed up flyers indicating what we had to offer, and we established a connection with a wholesaler in a nearby town — whom we found by looking in the Yellow Pages; there were tons of them — and we went around and looked at his trees and they looked decent. We distributed the leaflets all around. We had our dorm room phone number on it, which turned out not to be totally legal.

But it all worked out real well. We ended up selling about 120 trees, and each of us made about $250. But we only sold for a ten-day period, and we weren't putting in any eight hours a day. Two of us would go on a run, and then the one or two others would stay in the room in case anyone called. We worked only a couple of hours each day. We all made good Christmas money, which was exactly what we had intended to do and we had enough money to buy presents.

The whole deal was very interesting because I was a freshman and didn't know Boston at all, and I learned a lot about it.

One of the things that really helped was that my older brother who lives in Maine had recently bought a beat-up old pickup truck, which he rented to us for a whole month for $200. It wasn't a very good truck — in fact, our friends called it the Death Truck — but it served our purposes. Without it we couldn't have done it.

It was a big, old, open-backed Ford. And we just threw the trees in the back. If they were still in bundles (of twos or threes) we could get as many as twenty trees in it, but if they had been unbundled they took up more room and we couldn't get as many in the truck. One of the problems is that people like to select their Christmas trees personally, so we had to bring along a bunch for them to select from. Of course, by the time we got to the end of our run we usually had some real dogs on the truck, and occasionally we came up with some very creative ways of selling them.

Next time we could do it better simply by buying more trees, because we made such a profit on them anyway that we could have the junky ones and still make money. It was definitely a first-year-type operation where you make a lot of mistakes. Because we didn't have the truck we didn't do it this year, but we are definitely thinking about doing it next year. And the guys who live in our old room and have our old phone number said that they got about ten or fifteen calls this December from people wanting to know if we were going to be selling trees again. It would be a real easy thing to create repeat business. It could get quite big.

Another good thing about this deal was that it was just a little side business. We didn't have to bother to get incorporated, or anything like that. If we had tried to set up on the street and sell, it would have been different.

The key to the deal was the delivery. And we had someone who'd lived there and known it was a problem.

You learn a lot as you go. Initially, we thought we
would have to buy about two hundred trees. But luckily
we didn't do that, because it turned out we were able —
because the guy liked us — to go and buy them when we
needed them, when we had orders, because calls would
come in every day. So we didn't have to commit ourselves
to buying a specific number.

The guy we bought from was very busy. He had people
coming in from Pennsylvania in eighteen-wheelers, buying five hundred trees. And here we were with our pitiful
little order of twenty trees at a time. We were his small-
est customer by far.

We sold our trees for twenty to thirty bucks, an average of twenty-five bucks. Our flyer said $18, $20, $22,
$24 — something like that. We had some big trees, really
nice ones, that we sold for $30, and people were very
willing to pay it.

Originally, we thought we would have to cut our prices,
but it turned out that because we delivered, people were
perfectly willing to pay what we charged. And we were
competitive with some of the suburban areas. At the big
marketplace in downtown Boston, Faneuil Hall, they
were charging $30, $40, and $50! What people liked was
that for the same price or less they didn't have to go out
at all.

All in all it was a really good deal.

**GAME PLAN   To Sell Christmas Trees Door to
Door**

A. Market: "Targeted" individuals, in sections of
    Boston, who did not have a way, except via
    subway, to transport a Christmas tree.

    1. Approach: The use of flyers hand delivered to
        the targeted market.

2. Price: The price was established at the going market rate, but with free delivery as the incentive to the consumer.

3. Timing: The two weeks before Christmas, which proved to be adequate, but an early start would have been preferable.

B. Competition: Christmas tree stands located near subway stops; only the one at Fanueil Hall was seen as real competition, but it did not offer delivery.

C. Goods and Overhead

1. Materials: A local supply of inexpensive Christmas trees.

2. Equipment: A truck was necessary for the pickup and delivery of the goods.

3. Facilities: The dorm phone was used to receive calls for orders.

D. Capital: Money was needed to cover the cost of Christmas trees and to pay for flyers and delivery. The cost of the trees, although ordered in quantity, was softened by paying for only a dozen or so trees at a time. Delivery immediately followed the pickup of the Christmas trees, so cash flow was not a problem. For an initial investment of under $100, this deal quickly went into the black after the first delivery.

E. Regulations: Due to the small size of the operation, legal regulations and formalities were ignored.

F. Risk

1. Financial: This was minimal because the cash-flow system prevented serious risk.

2. Hidden Risks: The quality of the trees is an important factor. Make sure you know and trust your supplier.

G. Time Commitment: This type of operation involves little time and can be done easily for quick cash.

H. What's Involved

1. Finding an inexpensive, and not too distant, supply of Christmas trees.
2. Having use of a truck or setting up a means for delivery.
3. Advertising the availability of this service to the potential market.
4. Having a means of taking orders.
5. Delivery.

The beauty of the Christmas tree deal is that it is so simple. You may have to get a license (check that in your own area by calling the town counsel or city attorney's office) but the amount of money needed to get started is not great, plus you have the option of asking for a down payment, which would return some of your cash right away. The sooner you plan and outline all the details, the better your operation will function, but, as you have seen, it can be done as late as Thanksgiving and still work. A truck is necessary, but you don't have to buy one. (Check out the local truck rental prices, which are usually reasonable, if you don't have a friend with a truck.) A good flyer or poster (or both) is important, but you don't have to distribute them yourself. Things worked out very well for Gerrit and company, but it wouldn't be a bad idea to make sure you have a backup supplier for the trees just in case something goes wrong. Another idea that our friends didn't use but that would be a big help is to use a phone-answering machine so that interested potential customers can reach you without your having to stay near the phone. It might seem that this idea would work best in crowded metropolitan areas, but there are lots of smaller cities and towns whose citizens would welcome such a service, especially senior citizens. Finally, if you like people, Christmastime is a great time to be providing a service.

A Fellow Trekker and Summertime (House) Painter

Emmett O'Donnell was a nineteen-year-old freshman from Belmont, Massachusetts, at the time of the big Christmas tree deal. A kindred spirit, he had worked one summer, at age sixteen, for the minimum wage ($2.65) as a packer in a nuts and bolts factory — where he thought he would go nuts and bolt. Since then he had had a few other hourly wage jobs, but in the summer of 1981, encouraged by his tree-selling experiences the previous winter, he took the plunge and operated his own house-painting business in Newport, Rhode Island.

Last summer two of my roommates and I started a house-painting business in Newport, Rhode Island. But we had hardly started when they had to drop out for other opportunities and I found myself totally on my own. Newport is the beautiful resort town where the movie *High Society* was made, but we had a little ragtag apartment on the wrong side of town.

I was doing exterior house painting, which I had never done before, though I had done some painting around my parents' house and knew, basically, primers, and the difference between oil and latex, and what was needed. During the months of March, April, and May, I went to Newport on weekends and leafleted the whole place, and I took ads in the local newspaper. I used my school's name, hoping that would add an air of responsibility. I spent about $80 to $100 on 5,000 or 6,000 colorful leaflets, and took those around on Saturdays, and the calls just started rolling in.

Eventually I got so much work that at one point I had to hire a couple of kids to keep up with the demand. And

I had to turn down a lot of jobs at the end of the summer because I had to go back to school. I think that if I had wanted to stay there I could have competed with the painting companies.

The way I would work it — to make the most money personally — was to work as hard as I could for the shortest period of time. If the job should have taken me two weeks, I would do it in one week by working ten hours a day, and make a much bigger profit. Then I might take a little time off the next week before starting another job. I remember doing a couple of houses for $1,500, each one in a week, with maybe a couple of hundred dollars in expenses, so I was walking away with $1,200 to $1,300 in my pocket.

People should remember that painting the outside of a house does not take much skill. The skill comes in trying to survive the boredom; if you can do that you've licked the battle. It was nothing. All I had to do was figure in my paint costs, and the number of hours, roughly, that I thought it would take me (and a helper I would hire at a certain rate) and make my bid. I overbid at first, which turned out to be okay because I had so much work, but eventually I learned how to bid; by the end of the summer I was very competitive. Usually I asked the people for a couple of hundred dollars in advance for the paint and the brushes and scrapers, and whatever else I needed, and that was no problem. I would ask for the remainder of the first half when I was half finished with the job, and the rest when I was all done. That way they could see how I was doing and tell if they were satisfied before I was all finished with the job.

I bought an old AMC Jeep, kind of a Jeep station wagon, a 1969, with holes in the floor, that did about twenty-five miles an hour maximum speed, for a couple of hundred dollars; at the end of the summer I sold it for $150. I had two big ladders that I'd borrowed, one from my father and another from an uncle, and I tied them to the roof. I didn't fix up the truck or paint a sign on it, but I think I probably should have to attract more customers.

I think I made about $4000 net over the summer, working from May 25 to August 25; because I was living on my own I had a lot more expenses.

Now I was lucky; because of connections I had two jobs, two houses to paint, before the summer even started. But that wasn't a necessity. The jobs sort of rotated: you'd do somebody's house, or even just talk to him about doing it, and he'd say you should go over and talk to his neighbor whose house really needed it. That really helped.

There was room for ten more kids like me to start the same business in Newport. One of the reasons is that I did it in the summer and in a summer resort area. That was important. There are tons of people who come and want to clean up their summer places every year, whether it's the Cape or Newport or Martha's Vineyard. I think it would be difficult to do in a city, but down in a sort of cottagey area, where the people have to have their places painted every couple of years, it works. And they have the money. Plus, they're on vacation. They don't want to paint their houses during vacation, so they're willing to pay you.

Of course the painting business depends on the weather; you can't paint when it rains. But if I did it again, and I probably will this coming summer, I would probably do even better because now I know how to bid.

It's the kind of job that girls can do too. Sometimes you run into a helper who is afraid of heights, but I used to do all the monkey work myself, so that was no problem. It was just a summer job, and one that anybody could do anytime, except in the coldest weather, without a lot of money or special experience.

GAME PLAN To Establish a Painting Company

A. Market: Newport, R.I., a wealthy summer resort area with mansions and "cottagey" homes.

   1. Approach: Distributing leaflets and advertising in local newspapers.

2. Price: Price quotes were based on an approximation of $.60 per square foot for exterior work and $.40 per square foot for interior work. These prices are inclusive of all materials. If a customer supplies the goods, deduct his costs from the approximate price to arrive at a fair estimate.
3. Timing: This particular business operated during the summer months; however, a year-round business could be developed using the same techniques.

B. Competition: The high number of summer vacation homes would have allowed for at least ten more companies the size of Emmett's.

C. Goods and Overhead
1. Materials: Paint, brushes, and rollers.
2. Equipment: Ladders, scrapers, and transportation.

D. Capital: Several hundred dollars may be needed, depending on one's access to free equipment.
1. Cash Flow: The customer pays for all materials up front, then half the total is due about midway through the job, with the balance due on completion.

E. Risk
1. Financial: This venture involves the leverage of *backs,* not bucks, so the risk is minimal.
2. Word of Caution: Determine the client's satisfaction as the work progresses, in order to "troubleshoot," and to avoid costly misunderstandings.

F. Time Commitment: The hours are flexible, with plenty of time to enjoy vacations, unless you are trying to make the greatest amount of money in the shortest period of time.

G. What's Involved
1. Securing the equipment.
2. Soliciting customers.
3. Giving estimates.
4. Hiring workers.
5. Painting — watch out for boredom!
6. Earning about $4,000 in three months.

One of the best ways to get started in a business like house painting is to serve a term as an "apprentice," and watch how the "boss" does it. Emmett admits that things would have gone even more smoothly if he had done so (though they still worked out very well for him). A problem that plagued him, and would present difficulties for any first-timer, is that of bidding. How much to ask? An experienced paint salesman, any paint store or hardware store should have several, can give you some idea of how to measure the size of the house, the condition of the surface (density is very important because certain surfaces seem to drink the paint right out of the can), and the degree of difficulty involved (such as, to use Emmett's phrase, the amount of "monkey work" you'll have to do). But trial and error will probably end up being your best teacher.

It is vitally important to remember that word of mouth will be your best form of advertising, so you cannot afford to do less than your best work in the hope of doing a big volume of business. If you skimp on your initial customers, the word will get around. But if you do a good solid job for a fair price, your customers will probably do a better job than you of lining up new business.

Emmett didn't put a sign on his truck, but if you have a truck, and it is going to sit in front of the customer's house all day while you paint, it would be a shame not to use its sides for advertising. Even if you don't have an official company, you can at least list your name and phone number. And remember, business cards are a very cheap but very good investment.

Ceramic Pumpkins

Mike Steiner is a twenty-year-old, third-year Economics major from Albany, New York. He didn't get involved in any noticeably entrepreneurial deals prior to college, but once there, he found himself more and more interested in such activities. Mike's parents had stressed that "college should be a learning experience" and he took that admonition broadly.

He tried, and failed, to sell crowd caps, in which he and a partner had invested rather heavily. ("Even though we put on our thickest *Haaavahd* accents, we couldn't get the caps to move when we tried to sell them at hockey games.") He and another partner took over management of their house's basement grille, which served mainly hamburgers late at night to those who were still hungry or had been dissatisfied with that night's house meal. ("If it was a bad dinner, I still kind of smiled while I ate it, because I knew it meant we'd have good business that night in the grille.") Once he got to running it alone he managed some innovations — such as his thoroughly unprofessional, and unartistic, illustrated ads, which drew a lot of business: "I think most people just came in to see the idiot who had drawn the things" — and his profits rose. One of his first promising ventures came about because of his membership in the Harvard Entrepreneurs Society.

This idea came from a member of the Entrepreneurs club. In fact it was Ed. He told me he'd been driving through Washington and had stopped at a filling station; while he was there he saw this ceramic pumpkin, you know, stone, and he bought one and brought it back up here and tried to introduce it at a meeting of the Entrepreneurs club. And, God, from what I hear he never got more flak about anything than he did about that. They really teased him. I mean, it *is* kind of silly looking.

But what impressed him was that when he'd been by that same filling station earlier that day there had been about fifty of them, but by the time he stopped in the afternoon all but one were gone. So he really thought it had potential.

I went back to his room to see the thing, and I thought it was sort of cute, and a good idea. So I agreed to take it around to a few stores to see what kind of interest there was. I mean, the idea was that you bought one of these and put it in your window year after year and you never had to buy another fresh pumpkin. It had a cover in the shape of a hat, it was durable, and you could use it as a cookie jar, a candle holder, or even a planter. You could do anything with it. Just use your imagination.

He gave me the thing right around Halloween time, maybe a day or two before, so we were too late to sell them that October (we didn't even know where to get them yet!) but we could get a good idea of whether or not they were salable. I took the "model," the only one we had, and went into three or four flower shops. Just to see. Of course I thought I was going to be laughed out the door. I walked up to the manager of the first store and said, "Do you think you'd be interested in buying a product like this?" He looked at the thing, and he said, "Yeah. It's kind of cute. I like that thing." He said he wouldn't order it this year, but he would take a couple dozen if I came back next year.

I went to a couple of other places, and three out of the four said they would take them. I told them it sold to the public for $15, and I could probably sell it to them for about $6.00. We had no sure idea of what we could get them for, but that wasn't the thing. It was to see if they liked the idea of a ceramic pumpkin.

So then I went into one more store and the guy started laughing at me. He said, "Why don't you stand out on the corner and sell those stupid things yourself?" And I was saying, "Yeah, well, sure, I guess I'm on my way out of *here.*" Just as he was turning away, a lady came up to me and said, "Where did you get that? It's so cute!"

With a smirk on my face, I said I was just seeing if there was a market for these things. She said, "I'd definitely be interested in buying one of those. It's a shame they're not for sale yet." So I thought there might be a market for them.

I went home and began to try to find the guy who had made this pumpkin. But I couldn't find him. Ed gave me a bunch of leads, and I called Texas, California, Wisconsin, I don't know, wherever, and I couldn't find any companies that made ceramic pumpkins. Then I tried the Boston Yellow Pages, but I didn't have too much luck. I found a couple of places that said they made them, but for $12 or $15 wholesale. One guy really bugged me. He thought he was God's gift to ceramic pumpkins. "Yeah," he said, "I make those things. But who are you and what's your interest?" By the end of the conversation it turned out he didn't make them at all, and just before I hung up he said, "Hey, if you ever find any, let me know. I might like to sell 'em too."

What this did was motivate the hell out of me. I *had* to find this pumpkin! So I went over to the Business School, where they have a list of businesses, and looked in their list of ceramic places around the country. I got a list of about twelve, and went back to my room and started dialing numbers.

Every time I'd get the same thing: "Well, we don't do anything like that. That's not what we do." But I would keep saying, "Do you have any idea where I might be able to find this?" And they'd say, "Naaah." Finally, I got to the last name, literally the last name. It was in California, and I said, "Listen, I'm really frustrated." And I was; one afternoon I'd even asked my father to help. We were out drinking together, and he suggested that one of his friends might help, but it turned out, as usual, that nobody wanted to deal in small volume.

Anyway, I reached this last place in California; a real nice lady answered the phone and said, "We don't do anything like that." I said, "Please, you gotta help me. I really gotta find these things." I was *begging*. I was beginning to feel paranoid, as if everybody was holding out on me! She went away from the phone for a while, and when she came back she said, "Look, I just asked a couple of friends, and here's the name of a place you might want to try."

I dialed the number, which was also in California, and sure enough they make these things — and they make 'em real cheap. The guy quoted me a price between $2.00 and $2.25. I said, "Great!"

The guy was supposed to send me a prototype. But two weeks later, three weeks later, nothing. I would call, and he'd give me some excuse, but still the pumpkins didn't come, and I was getting worried because I had to get started marketing these things. By this time, it was January or February and I was still waiting for these pumpkins to show up. This guy was really, really bumming me out.

Finally I got a call from the guy, who said, "I can't send you the pumpkins." I said, "Why not?" and he said, "Well, that would be infringing on our salesmen in the area, and it's just against our policy to do something like that. I'm really sorry, Mike."

I couldn't believe it. I hung up, called Ed, and said, "Ed, the guys aren't going for it, what do I do?" Write a letter, he said. Tell them you promise to give them 50 percent down, tell them everything, just tell them you want the pumpkins for prototypes. So I wrote them a letter. No response. Ever.

Finally I called back again and talked to this same guy, and I said, "What's your deal? Why won't you sell them to me?"

He said, "Look, I have a boss. You'd better talk to him."

It turned out that this guy I'd been dealing with wasn't the head of the company at all. He was a *salesman* — which is why he didn't want me selling any pumpkins anywhere because it would be competition for him.

I got the name of the boss and called him and he was psyched for it! "Terrific. We don't have anything out in

the East and we really want to get started out there.
We'll help you out. What do you need?"

We just got the prototypes recently, and they're terrific.
I don't know exactly how we're going to market them —
whether we'll hire a bunch of people — probably not —
and how many we're going to order — but I'm working
on all that right now. I've really learned a lot doing all of
this.

And I'm still learning. You never know what will happen. For all I know the truck on the way out here is
going to tip over and all the pumpkins are going to
crash. I don't know. It's still in the development stage,
but I'm having a great time.

GAME PLAN   To Wholesale Ceramic Pumpkins

A. Market: Retailers, or other potential wholesalers,
    or people who represent gift items and specialty
    items.

    1. Timing: The orders will vary, depending on the
        various buying schedules of the consumers.
        Because this is a wholesale business, orders
        will be obtained year round. Due to the limited
        production capability of the manufacturing
        plant, it is necessary to order at least three
        months in advance to guarantee supply.

    2. Price: This product has a fantastic markup for
        the retailer, because of the extremely
        inexpensive production and wholesale costs.

B. Competition: There is no competitor on the East
    Coast who is capable of supplying the ceramics at
    anywhere near the same wholesale price.

C. Goods and Overhead

    1. Materials: Brochures are necessary to send to
        potential buyers. Ceramic pumpkins must be
        ordered in advance from the manufacturer.

2. A means of delivering the ceramics to the East Coast and distributing them from there.
3. Facilities: A central address and phone number at which to receive orders and inquiries. Also, a place to store the goods until the date of distribution.

D. Capital: Probably about $10,000 will be needed the first year for the ceramics and delivery, which represent about 95 percent of the cost.
   1. Cash flow: There will be at least a thirty-day wait for payment and in some cases up to ninety days, depending on the specific terms negotiated.

E. Risk
   1. Financial: Once the venture is established and the entire procedure understood, the risk should be minimal, but the first year could show a slight loss.
   2. Hidden dangers: The possibility of the truck smashing does pose a risk, but insurance would cover the cost of the invoice. Good luck, Mike!

F. Time Commitment: The time involved will probably be heavy throughout the first two years, especially during peak periods. After the first couple of years, depending on his initial success, Mike should have to put in little time except to count his money.

G. What's Involved
   1. Securing an exclusive right from the supplier to market and distribute this product on the East Coast.
   2. Obtaining purchase orders.
   3. Ordering the goods well in advance to guarantee product.
   4. Delivery.

H. Ultimate goal: An efficient network of manufacturer's representatives bringing in tens of thousands of dollars.

When you read that $10,000 is necessary for the initial investment, you may think we put Ceramic Pumpkins in the wrong section. That amount, however, is what we suggest you should have if you wanted to turn this into a full-time, no-other-commitment-type business. We put this venture in the "Small" section because of the way that Mike got started, which was to use only one or two samples, which cost only about $200, including the long-distance calls, and take them around to merchants to see if there was a demand. Once Mike determined there was, he could decide just how heavily he wanted to get involved.

The reader can do the same thing, but the type of product is up to you. The point of the example is to show that you can learn how the wholesale aspect of merchandising works, and you can pick your own product. Any number of manufacturers out there, in all areas of the country, need people to push their products. And how much better it is when you own "a piece of the action."

"Free" Posters for $$$

Bob Keane, another Economics major, is a nineteen-year-old freshman from Buffalo, New York. He admits to having had "get-rich-quick" dreams for a long time. While in high school he designed and sold banners, and thought up a variety of other schemes, none of which actually made him money, much less wealthy. But he didn't stop dreaming. In his last year he got the idea of capitalizing on the popularity of the space shuttle when he read that NASA was letting the public purchase canisters that would be cargo on the shuttle, and thus whatever was inside would also have made the trip.

"I wanted to sell bumper stickers that read: 'This bumper sticker flew in space on the Columbia.' But then, fortunately before I went too far, I realized that there was no way of *proving* that they'd ever been in space! I still like the idea and wish there would have been some way of validating it. But anybody could *say* something had flown in space, and who could tell, so why buy it?"

Bob Keane has his life rather neatly planned, without being rigid about it, and won't mind at all if he ends up just like his father, a company president who helped build the company through his own initiative and not as someone else's employee. But first Bob has to finish school and try out a few more "schemes." His latest, which he started setting up during the end of his freshman year, sounds very good to us. It has to do with that staple of student apartment decor, the wall poster.

My venture is called RPP, Inc., which I took from the words *Retail Promotion Products*; it involves posters. I'm a big skier, I've worked in ski shops, and I've learned that the ski companies often give promotional posters to retail stores, where they're put up on the wall. Like, say, Salomon, or something. They're really nice-looking posters, and a lot of cusomers ask if they can have them when you are ready to throw them out.

There's no place that you can really buy them. I got mine because I worked in the stores, but I noticed that all my friends asked me where I'd gotten them.

So last year I started looking around, and I've called different corporations. I have five concrete offers to let me distribute their posters. I'm not doing just skiing. These companies don't make that many posters in large quantities. They might make only a thousand for the thousand largest retailers, which means there are not that many around. Or a few of the companies, like Lange boots, give them away to anyone who asks for them, so they didn't want some people to have to pay while others get them free.

I've gone to these companies and offered to buy the posters for half their cost, and explained that what I sell will be advertising for them because the posters will go up in college dorms and game rooms, and I'll take care of everything.

I've gotten Dina Latarsky's K-2 skis, some of the other bigger brands, and Labatt's beer. Budweiser beer, which I've been trying to get, is a little edgy because I'm only going to be doing five states — Massachusetts, New Jersey, New York, Connecticut, and Rhode Island — and not the whole country. So I'm not sure about that. Also, Budweiser does sell some through magazines, like the one on the back page of *Rolling Stone,* which is a scene of a city with a beer can coming through at the top and everyone looking up; it's sort of surrealistic.

I've just gone after specific posters that I thought people would like, based on what my friends and I like. I've considered taking polls, but I haven't done it yet. Now I'm starting to go to the retail stores. I've talked to retailers I know, and they've said they'd be interested in buying them.

In four of the cases I've got an exclusive contract for two years, because I realized that, once I started doing it, others might say, "Why don't *I* start selling them?"

I know what the posters are going to cost me, which varies, so I know I can make a good profit by selling them to the stores at $3.50. The stores will sell them for $5.00 or so. The poster shops and college stores usually buy in quantities of 200 or 250. No huge sums are involved, but there are a lot of shops around, and I've got a big area. The problem is how I'm going to get everywhere. I'm considering going to places like Boston or New York, where there are a lot of young people, and getting a student in one of the colleges to be my representative. I'd give the agent a 10 percent commission; someone who sold, say, a thousand dollars' worth of posters or whatever would be making a lot of money. And that really wouldn't take much profit away from me.

I think the big problem is going to be distributing them, which is why I haven't gone out to do it all at once. My plan is to start in smaller quantities and work up. I've told most of the suppliers that I'll try to go for about a thousand at first.

Another problem is the capital. My father's in business, and I've talked it over with him a few times. He thinks that I can go to the stores and actually get — I had already thought of this too — the exact orders and ask them to give me, say, one-half as a down payment. Which I would use as *my* down payment. When they pay the balance, I'll pay the balance. That may not be the traditional way of doing business, but it has been done many times. Usually if you have a 50 percent down payment people won't have that many qualms about it.

The backlog at the printer's, at least at the one place I checked, is about twenty days, which isn't too long a time to wait. I'll be going around this summer, in my off-time, trying to get some posters so that I can take advantage of the back-to-school rush for posters, when students want to decorate their rooms.

I've inquired into the different mailboxes you can rent, and some of them, in addition to mail, will take shipments of merchandise and hold them for up to five days. As for storage for a couple of weeks or months, when I get into that I think I'll end up having to rent a place. Since running a business out of a dorm room is in theory illegal, I'll probably have to get an answering service.

I've got this pretty well thought out, and the only money I've spent so far is for phone calls. In the past I've always tried to get rich quick; I've had schemes and thought them out and then figured they weren't going to work. I've never really gone out and earned a lot of money, or lost a lot. But I think this one can work.

As far as long-range plans are concerned, I'd like to graduate from here and then take off maybe two years and work in a manufacturing company setting or possibly in investment banking. Or something like that, just to get the feel of it. Then I'd like to come back to the Business School after, say, two or three years. After that my plans are to go into business again, get a little money, buy into a small company, and work that up from there. Which is essentially what my father did.

GAME PLAN   To Wholesale Promotional Posters

A. Market: Principally college students (skiers and nonskiers), who would use them to decorate their rooms.

1. Approach: To set up commissioned wholesalers to distribute to stores principally located near colleges and universities.
2. Price: Make a good profit wholesaling at $3.50 an item that would retail for $5.00.
3. Timing: The beginning of the school year would be the ideal time to sell these posters at retail since students will be moving into dorms and purchasing posters to liven up their walls. Students represent a substantial segment of the poster market.

B. Competition: Some companies sell, or issue free on request, posters planned for sale; but many of the posters are currently produced for limited promotion and are unavailable to the general public.

C. Goods and Overhead

1. Materials: Posters will be purchased at one-half the cost of producing them.
2. Equipment: A means of distributing the posters is necessary.
3. Facilities: Warehousing facilities may become a necessity. Also, in this case, the problem of receiving orders needs to be solved.

D. Capital: To eliminate cash-flow problems and to prevent up-front investment, a down payment of 50 percent will be due with the orders.

E. Risk

　　1. Financial: This should be nonexistent with 50
　　　　percent down required on orders. But if this
　　　　venture never becomes operational, the costs,
　　　　for phone calls, brochures, and other materials
　　　　obtained to initiate the business, would
　　　　represent a loss.
　　2. Hidden Dangers: The possibility that orders
　　　　taken on consignment may be returned due to
　　　　lack of demand or oversupply.

F. Time Commitment: This business involves an initial
　　time period to arrange for the delivery of the
　　posters. This may be a time-consuming process,
　　not because it involves a great deal of work, but
　　because the mechanism for establishing such a
　　relationship travels slowly through the bureaucracy
　　of companies. Once he has established himself,
　　Bob's role should be minimal — and profitable.

G. What's Involved

　　1. Setting up the numerous arrangements to
　　　　secure the posters.
　　2. Marketing the posters to wholesalers or
　　　　retailers.
　　3. Delivering the goods to market.

Posters is an example of an entrepreneurial venture
that is classically simple, the kind of deal that makes
people say, "Why didn't *I* think of that?" which is, of
course, a tribute to its worth. What made Bob different
is that he realized what he had right in his hand, so to
speak. Readers should ask themselves if they may be
overlooking opportunities close to home: if you work for
a fast-food chain, for example, would they like to set up
a small outlet on your campus? Or would they like to
branch out into delivery service? You won't know until
you ask.

Another asset of Bob Keane's experience is that he learned how relatively simple it is to go to a large outfit and ask for an exclusive agreement to market their product in a given area. There is nothing magical about it. But if you don't ask first, you'll lose out. Don't make the mistake of saying to yourself, "Oh, someone else has probably thought of that already." Find out!

Notice also that once this kind of a business is set up (and especially if it has been set up carefully and well), it almost literally runs itself. And you are free to use the money it brings in to try new ventures.

Introducing the World's Youngest Adidas Dealer

Jaime Wolf, like Bob Keane, was just finishing his freshman year when we interviewed him for this book. Eighteen years old, from Pomona, New York, he is a Visual and Environmental Studies major. Unlike almost everyone else mentioned in this book, he had already made his entrepreneurial mark *before* he went to college.

My major is Visual and Environmental Studies, but in English that means film and literature. Visual and Environmental Studies can be film, photography, studio art — which is painting, printmaking, and architecture. It's a pretty wide department, a neat one. I'm going to combine stuff that I like about literature with the stuff that's in film and media. I also like to write.

My "area of expertise" is sporting goods. When I was thirteen years old — I was a seventh-grader — suede sneakers, running shoes, and all that stuff, were just beginning to come into fashion. The big names were Nike and Adidas. It was time for me to get a new pair of sneakers. I was tired of wearing old Keds every year. Other people were wearing different kinds of sneakers. I liked the way some of them looked, but instead of just going out and buying them, I wanted to figure out which ones were the best.

So I wrote away to several companies for their catalogues to see what kind of inventory they had and what price and style range they stocked. I went to a number of sporting goods stores and just looked at the sneakers and how they were made and what they were built for. I talked to friends and people I knew who wore different kinds of sneakers and asked them what they liked about them.

Also, I did a whole mess of research, and I found out that, at least in my opinion, Adidas had just about the best sneakers in every category — comfortable, nice-looking, and incredibly functional; I mean, you look at all the Olympic athletes and that's all that most of them, from all of the countries, wear. Not only that, but the sporting wear Adidas made, the clothes, were also far beyond anything anyone else made. They didn't make just sneakers, they made a whole line of products. Everything was consistently nice. I liked the way their line looked; it was comfortable, it was neat. I was pretty amazed.

Now I wasn't any more fashion-conscious than any other suburban person. I was the same jeans and T-shirt person I am now. My interest was just curiosity, I guess, but I was athletic, and maybe that, rather than fashion, was what got me going. I was a tennis player, and a basketball player, and also baseball, so I was interested as an athlete and as a consumer.

I figured, "Gee, a real good way to make money would be for me to become an Adidas dealer!" If I could get the stuff at wholesale, I could sell it to all the people I knew at school and my tennis league and basketball league. I could make money that way, as well as being able to get my clothes wholesale; the Adidas line, while it was very good, cost a little more than I was used to paying.

I wrote a letter to Libco, in New Jersey, which was one of the five distributors for Adidas in the United States. I addressed it to the sales manager, because I didn't know who else to address it to. I said, "I'm thirteen years old and I think your stuff is the best stuff made, and I'd like to become an Adidas dealer." I proposed a way for me to compete with all the local sporting goods stores, which carried only certain stuff in the catalogue — I would sell at a 10 percent discount.

They wrote me back a nice letter that said, "While we admire your mature business sense," etc. — it was a praiseful letter because they'd never received anything like that from a thirteen-year-old person before — but "you can't become an Adidas dealer because you don't have a store, you don't have anyplace to store the inventory," and, in big letters, "Adidas cannot be sold at a discount!"

I was persistent. I wouldn't take no for an answer. I called them, and I said, "Well, gee, maybe I can't become a dealer, but can I make an appointment to come and see you at your office?" And they said sure. So I left school early one day and went to New Jersey with my father, a couple of hours' drive, and saw the warehouse and the offices and everything.

They really liked me. A vice president took time off and showed me all around the warehouse, gave me some clothes, T-shirts. He saw that I knew all about this stuff, and he tried to set me up with the local sporting goods dealer near my house. The local guy said okay. I was going to sell out of his inventory, as a little independent, and split the profit with him. But, as it turned out, he really wasn't too enthusiastic about it because he saw me as creating competition and taking away people who would normally buy from him. He didn't receive me too well; he didn't even want to give me stuff for myself at wholesale.

So I called up my friend the vice president and told him the guy wasn't interested. He finally said, "Look, you need anything, just send it to us and we'll fill your order." I got myself an account with Adidas when I was thirteen years old.

One of the reasons I could do that at that age was that I've always had a certain amount of self-confidence. And I was always athletic. I was a good tennis player. I teach now. I'd participated in a number of programs locally, so I knew a lot of people.

For a couple of years in junior high school I sold stuff

to friends, and it was kind of low-key because I felt that was the way the vice president wanted it; he was my friend, doing me a favor. I did this for a couple of years. I started going to sporting-goods shows in New York City and I became friendly with other people who represented other companies. I could have gotten an account at Nike; in fact I think I had one for a while. I also started stringing tennis racquets and doing things like that, odds and ends.

I made a nice amount, say, around $200 a month during school in the better months. Again, I wasn't pushing it. It was peanuts compared to what most of the guys around here get, but it was okay for someone fourteen or fifteen years old. I probably could have made a lot of money in the summers, but I went away summers.

If I have time I'd like to set up something with sporting goods here, because I really like it a lot. Instead of a sporting-goods store though, I think I'd like to open just a shoe store that would have a wild kind of inventory, with shoes no other people have, that would attract business into the store. Adidas makes things like parachuting boots and car-racing shoes. They're for a very limited public, but carrying them kind of advertises the store. And if the store is designed nicely, people will come in. That would be pretty neat.

Adidas is a German company. At a sporting-goods show in New York I met the eighty-year-old woman who owns and runs the company. She's very nice, but she certainly doesn't look like she owns a multimillion-dollar company. I told her my story, and she just smiled. She said, "Very nice. Come to Germany and visit me and I'll show you around." I haven't been to Germany to see her, but I'd like to go.

Some readers may think that Jaime Wolf's experience is so special that there is little to be learned from it because they could never do what he did. Jaime disagrees strongly.

I think it's very easy for somebody to go into sporting goods. Racquet-stringing — tennis racquets, squash racquets, racquetball racquets — is something a lot of young people go into because it's not that hard to learn and the investment in a racquet-stringing machine is about $150 to $300 for a decent table model. You can make that back after the first ten or twenty racquets. Stringing nylon can earn you $7.00 or $8.00 a racquet, and gut a lot more. Some racquet stringers make $15 a racquet.

As for being an Adidas dealer, I don't know how many people could actually do that. I think I happened to be really lucky. It was not necessarily the result of any great skill of mine, but just the right circumstances. I guess I used the right words in my letter. But somebody who is interested enough in sporting goods to know the market, to get himself an account with one dealer or another and be able to go to a trade show where he can meet people — introduce himself and say, "Hi, I'm Johnny So-and-so and I'm fourteen years old but I'm already making $50 a week selling this, but think what I could do for you because I'm involved with this racquet club and I go to this junior high school and I know the school store" — can do all right.

People who are in corporations love these kinds of stories because it's great PR for their product. So, it can be done. I know a couple of people who were selling T-shirts and they did all right. Sporting goods is not a bad place to start because if you start with only a little capital you can keep reinvesting more and more until you get to the point where you may need large capital, but it won't make any difference because you'll *have* it.

GAME PLAN To Retail Sporting Goods to Athletic Friends

A. Market: Friends and schoolmates who are athletically inclined.

   1. Approach: To be low key by selling to friends.
   2. Price: Prices were set by Adidas.
   3. Timing: Year round, based on the needs of friends.

B. Competition: The local sporting-goods store did not compete since the target market was "supplier-sensitive."

C. Goods and Overhead
   1. Materials: Sporting goods were purchased wholesale.

D. Capital: Inventory purchased on an as-needed basis, so moderate initial capital is required.

E. Time Commitment: Problems arose during the formation which involved a slight time delay. The lack of cooperation the local retailer exhibited toward assisting the establishment of a potential competitor is only natural, but from the eager marketer's viewpoint it is a costly waste of time. However, once the lines of supply were secured, the time involved varied, depending on the requests for merchandise, but was usually about ten hours per week.

F. What's Involved
   1. Establishing an account with a distributor.
   2. Filling the orders on demand from friends.

Obviously, very few people can be "the youngest" at whatever they do. But as Jaime's experience proves, you can do a great deal by taking advantage of your own experience and your own interests. Ask yourself where you spend most of your "disposable income" (as the economists call it) and you may find you have an obvious lead to a money-making venture. As Jaime says, corporations know that these kinds of stories are "great PR for their product." His approach can be utilized for anything you buy; it doesn't have to be a sporting-goods product. Are you a fan of a certain line of jeans, or sweaters, or shoes, or automobile tires? Contact the manufacturers. Perhaps they'd welcome having an exclusive distributor in West Bend, Wisconsin, or Fort Smith, Arkansas, or Torrance, California. And remember this: if you truly believe in a product, you can be a far more effective salesperson.

A Different Kind of Film Deal

At the ripe old age of twenty, Monroe Trout talks about being at "the end of my career." He is not talking about business, however, but about basketball, for the six-foot-six-inch Trout is Harvard's starting center. With the National Basketball Association taking only about thirty former college players each season, Trout feels it is now time to get down to the business of business.

With his last year coming up, Trout, who is an Economics major from New Canaan, Connecticut, hasn't given up on his dream of playing in the NBA, or at least the chance of a year in Europe playing for a team over there, but he understands the odds. And he has been interested in business for a long time. As a boy he always liked to play Risk and Monopoly much more than other board games, and in high school he operated a coin and stamp business by mail — "until I got ripped off." Like so many of the rest of us, Monroe hates the idea of working for nothing more than an hourly wage.

I'm taking two business courses now, but when I came here I really didn't think much past basketball. But now I'm really into business. In fact, I don't have a set job this summer; I'm just going to do my own thing. I have a whole bunch of things planned, and I want to see which one takes off the best.

When I was a kid I did have a lawn business, and I sold stamps and coins, and I made quite a bit of money doing it until I got ripped off. I was about sixteen or seventeen, and I made about a couple of thousand dollars in a couple of weeks, but I gave this guy some stamps on consignment and he wrote me a bad check. I had dealt with the guy before, and he was always prompt, paid the money right away, but this time he ripped me off. That left a really bitter taste in my mouth. In fact, I just recently got my money back, and now I'm back into it and interested again.

I set up a little arrangement with a dealer in our town, and I can have access to his inventory at prices just a little above what he buys estates for. The beauty of working with this man is that I wouldn't have to put out any money at all. I'll just go all around New York and New Jersey, trying to sell these things to other dealers. That's what I did before and it worked out well for me. Right now the stamp market's way down; it's in bad shape. But I'm fascinated by stamps and coins. If the arrangement took off well I could make some decent money.

I'm also thinking of setting up a videotape business. Taping houses for insurance purposes, that sort of thing; taping weddings, golf tournaments, tennis tournaments. A lot of them are or could be followed by banquets and I'd like to be the caterer too — make the highlight film, hold the banquet, get the food, and show the film. They would be nice occasions, and that way I'd make money both from the catering service and from the film. I'm also thinking of filming a bunch of graduation ceremonies and selling the films for fifteen or twenty bucks. That's something I have to look into, because it would also be a good complement to film-booklet sales, which right now is my main business.

I'm a marketing agent for a company called Allied Photo Service. Basically, I buy film booklets from them. Each booklet has a hundred coupons in it and each coupon is good for a roll of Kodak color film. I, in turn, sell these booklets for $15 each, but I have a little leeway to fool around with the prices. The customers get a roll of film for each roll they get developed through Allied. Allied has excellent photo prices, and they do a great job, getting them out within twenty-four hours. The company is in Wisconsin, so you have to allow a couple of days for the mail; I get my film back in six days.

My competitors sell the booklets for thirty bucks, and their developing prices aren't as good. For instance, they charge $8.90 to get a thirty-six-exposure film developed, and I charge $7.80, which is what the company charges. The customers get the free roll of film in each case, but it costs them twice as much to buy the booklets from my competitors.

If you bought a twenty-four-exposure roll of Kodak film around here, not in a discount store, it might cost you about $3.60; to have it developed would be $8.00. You would pay $11.60 in all. With my booklet you get the film developed for $5.60, plus you get the free roll of film, so the whole deal costs you $5.60. Your saving is $6.00; do that three times and you've paid for the entire booklet. You can also give away the coupons as gifts.

I ran across this opportunity because I read a bunch of magazines — *Entrepreneur, Salesman, Venture,* all of them. I sent away to all these companies to learn about their little spiels — bumper stickers, all that stuff. I must have about three hundred letters. I purposely put myself on all those mailing lists to get information. I get about ten letters a day as a result. Most of it is bogus, like those "send a dollar and get a free gift" offers. That's a contradiction in terms, but they pull that stuff. It's amazing.

One of them was so bad it was really funny. It said, "Get 40 Beautiful Pastel Cotton Towels for $1.75." I sent in my $1.75, and two months later I got a very small package that contained little paper towels that I guess had 1 percent cotton, and they were different colors. But it was worth it just for the laughs my roommates and I got. I'm the only one I know who sends away for all this stuff. Most of my roommates think I'm crazy. But that was how I ran across the film deal. It's really an excellent company; since 1967 they've developed over $100 million worth of film a year.

My next step is to start selling the booklets in bulk, like one hundred at a time for nearly the wholesale prices. I'm going to contact a bunch of people who run flea markets, because I think the booklets would go over well there. I want to get on a good mailing list of flea-market sellers. I want to make up a form letter to send to all these people, saying that I'll give them excellent prices if they buy a hundred from me. They, in turn, can mark them up.

So, the basic ideas I'm going to start with this summer are the film idea — the coupon booklets — the videotaping, and the stamps and coins. I'm also going to try to get a little investment club going, stocks and stuff, but that would be pretty much nonprofit. If it does well I could put it on a commission basis, as Jimmy Carona does (see Book Three, Chapter 2).

I guess I'm as interested now in business as I was or still am in basketball. The only thing I won't like is that when I'm twenty-two, and it's time to end my career, I'll be right at my peak. I grew sort of late. I'm not growing taller anymore, but I'm still growing stronger, and I'd hate to quit at twenty-two. That's why I think I'm going to play in Europe for a while. Just think of all the business opportunities I'd run across!

GAME PLAN   To Retail and Wholesale Film-Coupon Booklets

A. Market

    1. Approach: Word-of-mouth exposure at the retail level. Also, direct mail solicitation to flea-market vendors to encourage a wholesale business.

    2. Price: The suggested price is $15 at the retail level, with discounted prices for wholesalers.

    3. Timing: This is a year-round business.

B. Competition: Competitors who offer an identical package do exist, but they charge double. This price differential should provide a substantial edge over competitors.

C. Goods and Overhead

1. A ready supply of inventory to meet retail orders is required by the supplier. Quantity purchases of film booklets yield significant savings to the wholesaler, encouraging marketing aimed at high-volume sales.

D. Capital: The distributor requires a minimum purchase to secure an exclusive sales territory. This can be handled by fronting the money for the booklets and approaching markets to liquidate the inventory and/or receiving purchase orders, then ordering the goods, which minimizes the risk.

E. Risk

1. Financial: That the inventory won't move.
2. Hidden Dangers: That the sponsoring company won't uphold its agreement. This can be a problem with many of the "get-rich-quick" schemes. In this case, the company has been in business since 1967 and does over $100 million worth of film developing a year. A quick check with the Postal Service, Federal Trade Commission's regional office, or local Better Business Bureau may circumvent a costly lesson.

F. Time Commitment: As with most commission sales deals, the time involved depends on the amount of activity desired or the personal goals of the salesperson involved.

G. What's Involved

1. Purchasing a quantity of film booklets and establishing an exclusive territory.
2. Selling the booklets to captive markets.
3. Expanding your sales network to penetrate sales territory.

Monroe's problem — to the extent he has one — is that he has too many things going for him. The film deal is one that anybody can try, but you had better have a fairly orderly mind and be good at following up on things for your customers. It is the kind of business that can make you money without too much effort once you have it going properly. But it is also the kind of business that can make you very good money if you keep on top of all the new deals and offers and specials.

Notice that most of the things Monroe Trout now looks on as business ventures are things that he got into originally as hobbies. In that sense he is similar to Jaime Wolfe, the youngest Adidas dealer. It pays to work in an area in which you have both interest and experience.

Another warning worth heeding is that if you want to represent a company in a field as highly competitive as film processing, you have to be as careful as Monroe was in checking out the product, the prices, and the reputation of the company you expect to be identified with.

"Killer" or Even Your Best Friend Won't Warn You

Walter Burr, one of the principals of Fuel Tech, is a twenty-year-old sophomore from the small Massachusetts Cape town of Mattapoisett, which is near New Bedford. Walter says that being involved in business "has come as somewhat of a surprise to me," but he shouldn't really be that surprised because as a teenager he was involved in entrepreneurial ventures. In the nation's capital (while working for Congressman Gerry Studds), he designed and sold a T-shirt, but had to leave Washington before he had time to sell his stock; he found the regional message less than an instant hit in Mattapoisett, "pop.

5,000." Also, while at Andover he and a friend wrote a twenty-six-page pamphlet on how to study history, but gave it away! (He did not approach it as a money-making venture.) But then, Walter's main interest *is* politics, so he may have had an ultimate, ulterior motive.

In addition to being involved in Fuel Tech, however, Walter was one of the students who set up and ran the famous, or perhaps infamous, game known as "Killer," which had the Harvard campus turned upside down on several occasions a year or so ago. (Recently, someone told us that the idea of "Killer" had been made into a television movie, but none of us has seen it as yet. Perhaps it ran into the same bad end as the game did at Harvard.)

I was involved last year in that game, that silly game. Three people — two other roommates and I — ran it. I guess the main reason we did it was to see what would happen; and the place went nuts!

People have said the game actually had its start at some other school, but I distinctly remember sitting in our living room the night we decided to do it, and I for one was not aware that it had been done someplace else. Perhaps my roommates were, or one of them was, but my impression was that it just sort of formed out of a mishmash of ideas and prior consciousness. Someone also said later that he had seen mention of it in *Newsweek* a year before, and maybe he had, but the rules we ended up with were totally different. They were all our own.

The rules were: for the two-dollar entry fee paid to us, every contestant got a plastic water gun (which they didn't have to load if they didn't want to) and a card with the name of their victim. Someone else would have a card with your name on it. You could "kill" your victim by just going up and saying, "Bang, you're dead." But the trick was that you couldn't have more than four witnesses to any killing for the entire length of the game. You had to shoot your prey when no one was around.

If you used up four witnesses just like *that,* it hurt your chances. But when you got close to the end you might actually put off a "killing" because you wanted someone to witness it, for proof. We also devised a way to get the word out that we had a secret plan to catch people if they cheated, and it was pretty effective. But of course we had no such plan.

People went nuts over the game. I was walking through Harvard Yard one night at three o'clock, and I saw two people. One was at the far end, running from tree to tree, and the other was stalking him. Now I hadn't been out drinking until three o'clock, and it wasn't just my imagination.

After a while, the freshman dean closed down the game. There was a rumor going around that it was because an intended victim, who was trying not to get "killed," had switched name tags on his door and someone else's, with the result that in the middle of the night a female proctor was awakened by a male standing over her bed, pointing a gun at her, and saying, "I'm going to kill you."

The truth was not quite that colorful. A student unlocked and ran into a proctor's room, and then ran back out, saying, "Oh, sorry, we're just playing Killer." I happened to learn from the grapevine that the person who had done that wasn't even involved in the game. He just used it for an excuse.

The proctor was female, but he didn't wake her in the middle of the night, though he probably did scare her. There was something about a confusion in keys. In any event, it didn't help the reputation of the game but it may have increased its popularity, or at least its notoriety.

Unfortunately, the proctor complained to the freshman dean's office, and the person there flew off the handle — unfairly, in my opinion, because they didn't check out the circumstances — and closed the game down. Opinion was always widely divided. A few of the faculty thought the game was great, and a few thought it was childish. Well, of course it's childish. But it was fun.

That was the end of game one. Then we got permission to have game two. And right in the middle of it, Reagan got shot. So we sort of faded it out.

We got lambasted in the *Independent,* a campus newspaper. The editors attacked the whole concept, and tried to read into it, "This is the class of 1984?"

The mechanics of the thing were that we would put up notices on a Thursday, and by Saturday we had two hundred people — at $2.00 each — wanting to play. The winner would get $100. It really took off. I was on the front page of the *Harvard Crimson,* which ran three articles. A *Newsweek* reporter came up to interview us, but when he went back he found they'd already done an article about a similar game at the University of Michigan about a year and a half ago, so that didn't go through.

Even though the second game had to be called off, we awarded the prize anyway. There was this girl who, as soon as the game started, just went out like wildfire and — "Bang, bang, bang" — she kept calling every ten minutes for a new victim. She ended up having "shot" twelve or thirteen people. And that's not easy to do when you can't have any witnesses. But it was during exam reading period and she got a lot of opportunities. We ended up losing money on that one.

It was incredibly popular. There are sixteen hundred freshmen in the Yard, and for a period of several weeks the game was the central topic of conversation.

GAME PLAN   To Conduct a Game with Cash Reward to Winner

A. Market: Freshmen students at Harvard College.

1. Approach: The use of posters to advertise the game.
2. Price: A $2.00 fee.

B. Competition: Numerous alternative forms of available entertainment, on and off campus, but the uniqueness of this venture precludes the need to worry about competition.

C. Goods and Overhead
   1. Materials: Water guns, flyers, and $100 for the cash prize.
D. Capital: A minimal investment for flyers was needed to attract participants. Once the number of players could be determined, cash was needed for the appropriate number of water guns, with $100 reserved to reward the winner.
E. Regulations: The campus administration made life difficult for students involved; possible disciplinary action could have been taken against the students for running an unsanctioned business on campus.
F. Risk
   1. Financial: With the exception of an outside authority disrupting the game plan, the risk appears to be minimal.
G. Time Commitment: Varies with the length of each game.
H. What's Involved
   1. Formulating the rules of the game.
   2. Advertising for participants.
   3. Policing the operating of the game.
   4. Rewarding the winner, with about $100 in prize money.
   5. Reaping about $100 in profit.

A game like "Killer" can be great fun *and* can make its operators some money. But it should be remembered that while you, as the operator-originator, may think of it as being a business deal, many (if not most) other people may think of it as only a game. Be careful.

3

Caution: A Rose Is Not a Rose Below Freezing, but a Mug Is Always a Mug

---

The success of the firewood deal made us think we could do anything. As we soon found out, we could not. Let our experience serve as a warning to you that some sows' ears don't really want to be silk purses.

By the time Valentine's Day arrived, Ed was in the mood for another deal, another killing. This time the subject was roses. He learned that the flower shops were selling roses for $60 a dozen! That shocked him, and the more he thought about it the more convinced he became that he could find a floral wholesaler who would sell him a lot of roses at a price low enough for him to resell them at far less than the going rate and still make a good profit.

Thinking ahead, Ed went downtown several mornings in a row to scout locations, deciding that the best place to sell the roses would be in front of the John Hancock Building, a monstrous office tower in downtown Boston. He and Bob Wade, another undergraduate who had worked with us on the firewood, figured they could get a lot of the executive types who worked in the Hancock Building to buy roses. So they went to the proper city office in Boston and got a wholesaler's license and a hawker's license, and then bought the roses from a floral wholesaler's market — 700 roses and 160 vases, at a total cost of about $1,000. The roses cost them $12 a dozen, so their potential profit margin looked very good.

The plan was to start selling on Friday morning, the day before Valentine's Day; they figured they would sell out by that night or certainly by the next morning. It didn't quite work out that way. The executives were either too cheap or too busy to buy any flowers on their way in to the office, and on the way out they were apparently too busy.

Ed and Bob arrived downtown at seven in the morning; by two that afternoon they had sold approximately $50 worth. And the roses looked as if they were going to die.

When the temperature gets below freezing, which it definitely did, roses die. So they had to borrow a car and keep it running and warm, and put the roses inside. They couldn't even display them, and had to call people over to the car window, saying, "Hey, want to buy some roses?" as though they were "hot" or something. But they definitely were not hot. In fact, Ed and Bob sold some roses that were frozen.

They sold that whole day and evening too. They sold until the theaters let out, hoping to catch some lovers on their way home, but that didn't work either. The thou-sand-dollar investment — part of which Ed had borrowed — was not looking too good.

Some readers may wonder why Ed took the rose deal downtown, why he didn't just stay at school and sell them there, but Ed had checked that out and figured it would not have worked. For one thing, we'd already had enough trouble with Harvard because of the firewood deal and didn't want any more. For another, there is a saying around school that "there's no love at Harvard," which we happened to agree with, so it made little sense to try to sell something as romantic as a dozen roses on campus. Ed did check out several of the other schools in the area, thinking about taking out ads in their papers, but he found that a number of them were closed for the weekend.

The next day Ed and Bob altered the plan and headed for Downtown Crossing, a large intersection where there are a number of big department stores, like Filene's and Jordan Marsh. But that didn't turn out to be such a hot idea either.

It started out just great. They weren't selling dozens, but were selling half dozens and lots of individual roses, and doing great. Then Boston's Finest, the cops, descended on them and told them they couldn't sell there. So they found another spot, a hosiery store where the manager let them sell out in front, and they sold $200 worth in a single hour. The store had a Valentine's Day display in the window, which made a perfect backdrop. But then the cops came along and told them they couldn't sell *there*.

One cop actually took out his billy club to make them move on when Ed said it was private property and that they had a right to be there. Ed was so mad he went and called the police station and complained about the guy.

Ed and Bob were getting kind of scared by that time, so they resorted to coming on like bums, real street bums, and almost begging people to buy, trying any kind of trick they could think of. But it was kind of strange, because people who got close enough could read their hawkers' licenses, which said "Harvard University." Some people asked if they went to Harvard; a couple of times they told people they were conducting a psych experiment. Shortly before that a cop had told them they were "vagabonds."

The only way Ed and Bob were able to salvage the deal was by working like crazy. What they had thought would be an easy day, maybe a day and a half, of leisurely selling turned into two full days of intense hawking. But finally they did break even. Ed says he made $40 and Bob $20, for two whole days, which is slightly better than breaking even — but only slightly. And in all that time, they sold only one full dozen, to a girl coming out of a play on Saturday night. And they had to sell that one at cost!

Bill was happy that he had decided to go skiing that weekend instead of getting in on the roses deal. But he got his lesson in overoptimism not long after. In his case the holiday involved was Saint Patrick's Day, a natural for someone named Haney, but that turned out to be his salvation, not his inspiration.

The product in this instance was beer mugs — glass beer mugs. The idea was to spoof the ubiquitous Harvard emblem which, with its Latin word "Veritas," adorns everything from key chains to chair backs. Bill's idea was to buy a bunch of beer mugs and have them silk-screened with the similar-sounding but fun-poking words, "Very Trashed."

With his roommates — and fellow Irishmen — Gerrit Nicholas and Emmett O'Donnell, he bought 180 mugs, at $1.79 each, which they planned to sell for $5.00. But the mugs went flat. No one was excited about them. A few parents bought them, mainly as souvenirs, but not many students seemed to want them. They managed to convince the manager of a store near the campus to stock a half dozen, and then they sent in four of their friends — with their money — to buy one each, which made the manager think it was a hot item. He ordered fifteen more.

"By Saint Patrick's Day," says Bill, "we had about a hundred of them left. They were stacked up in cases in our rooms, which aren't supposed to be used for such things. But then we had an idea. We had planned a big party for Saint Pat's anyway, so we told people if they bought a mug for $5.00 they could drink beer all night for nothing extra. There was some risk involved, because we were committed to buying three kegs of beer, and we could have been stuck with the rest of the mugs. But it worked like *that*! We sold a hundred and ten mugs in ninety minutes. So, what had looked like a disaster, a la roses, worked out okay. Not great, but okay."

And, as Ed recalls, "The party was terrific."

GAME PLAN   **To Retail Roses through Direct Sales**

A. Market: Individuals who wanted roses for Valentine's Day
   1. Approach: To hawk roses on street corners.
   2. Price: To sell at $24 per dozen, which was $36 cheaper than the going rate.
   3. Timing: February 13 and Valentine's Day, based on the tradition of exchanging roses as a symbol of love.

B. Competition: Alternative gift ideas due to the unusually high price of roses at florist shops.

C. Goods and Overhead
   1. Materials: 700 roses and 160 cases.
   2. Equipment: A means to transport the goods and to keep the roses from freezing.

D. Capital: Over $1,000 needed for the roses, vases, and regulatory licenses.

E. Regulations: A wholesaler's license from the state and vendor's licenses from the city and state.

F. Risk
   1. Financial: Roses are perishable, so a lack of consumer demand would result in excess merchandise, leading to unreclaimable loss of goods.
   2. Hidden Dangers: The weather, which threatens the life of the roses and the venture. Also,

regulatory laws that prohibited access to the targeted market.

G. Time Commitment: The entire operation, from start to finish, involved about sixty hours of work.

H. What's Involved
   1. Arranging for the wholesale purchase of the roses at least one month in advance.
   2. Selecting and implementing a sales program.

The roses deal is a wonderful example of a good idea that went all wrong. If you try a variety of money-making schemes, as we have, you will almost certainly run into your own roses deal. Even if you try only a few, you may run into roses when you least expect it. As you have seen, we tried to figure all the things that could go wrong ahead of time — even down to having an alternate selling site picked out. But it still went wrong because the weather killed us — and some of the roses!

A lot of retail selling deals sound terrific if you don't factor the weather into the equation. But if there is a driving, freezing rain beating down, and you are trying to get people to stop on their way into a warm arena to buy a T-shirt or a cap, you're asking for trouble. Try to plan what else you can do with the product, or when else you can sell it, if the weather turns sour on your big day.

Also, make sure you understand not only the letter of the law, but also the spirit of its enforcers.

GAME PLAN To Sell Beer Mugs

A. Market: Harvard students.
   1. Approach: Direct sales to students.
   2. Price: $5.00 per mug.
   3. Timing: Not intended to be time-sensitive; but Saint Patrick's Day worked a miracle.

B. Competition: All around us, but the "Very Trashed" inscription was unique.

C. Goods and Overhead
   1. Materials: 3 kegs of beer and 180 mugs.

D. Capital: Cash up front to purchase the mugs.

E. Regulations: (Once again) Harvard University's rule prohibiting conducting business out of a dorm room.

F. Risk
   1. Financial: Losses due to theft or breakage were possible, but in this case poor consumer demand proved to be the main problem.

G. Time Commitment: The most time-consuming aspect of this venture involved selling the goods, which lasted for weeks (until word of the planned party caused a rush on the mug market).

H. What's Involved
   1. Designing and purchasing the mugs.
   2. Selling the mugs.

In theory, a seller ought to be able to recover from a mugs-like deal more easily than one like roses. But that will not always prove to be the case if you have chosen a promotional or direct-sales item that nobody seems to want. There are ideas that just knock you out, that you think are irresistibly attractive or hilariously funny; but if your intended customers don't agree, you will have had it, and fast.

This is a perfect area in which to do a little "test-marketing." Try the idea on a few friends, or, better yet, on a few strangers; if they like it, and indicate a willingness to buy, then you are on safer ground. But it still wouldn't hurt to test the waters even further by having a prototype or a model that potential customers can react to. That way you will be able to protect the great bulk of your investment.

Good luck. But if all else fails, remember that old faithful — the going-out-of-business sale!

BOOK TWO

Medium or Not-So-Small Can Be Beautiful Too

1

Founding the Harvard Entrepreneurs Society or Dos and Don'ts for Starting Your Own Undergraduate $ Club

---

The success of the wood deal, plus the word-of-mouth reactions to roses and beer mugs, earned us the reputation as the people to see on campus if you wanted to get involved in a business deal. More and more students began to seek us out and ask our advice. To Ed, who'd been discouraged by the lack of enthusiasm and initiative on the part of many students he'd worked with, this change was particularly heartening. It made him begin to wonder if perhaps there weren't quite a few students, or at least a select few, who would benefit from some sort of undergraduate entrepreneurial association.

We started to talk about the possibility of a club. Harvard already had scores of them, everything from Hasty Pudding to Gay and Lesbian clubs. They all enjoyed the privilege of being allowed to put up posters and announcements, and having the use of university meeting rooms.

One of their biggest advantages was that clubs were allowed to raise money. Originally, we'd thought that the Harvard Entrepreneurs might be a club that could tap the alumni and get them to put some money in the club, which we could use for investment purposes, an approach used by a number of other clubs on campus.

As the winter of 1980–1981 began to wane, Ed became more and more excited about the idea of the club. He loved the idea of its being "Harvard-approved," but, as things turned out, that was the hardest part.

The first meeting on behalf of the club was between Ed and one of the deans in charge of student affairs, and in our view it did not go well. Ed came away so angry that he was determined to go straight to the press and reveal how Harvard blocked free enterprise, warn companies not to donate money to Harvard because of that, and tell why the whole thing didn't reflect the capitalist system. He was *steaming*. But Ed just wasn't about to let anything stand in his way, in the way of the Harvard Entrepreneurs club, which we thought was a very good idea.

What followed was an intricate and time-consuming dance. We tried to meet the requirements set by the dean, but when we did it seemed like he promptly set up new ones. Eventually, our persistence, which was mainly Ed's persistence, prevailed. But it was not done without a great deal of effort. For example, when told that he had to go out and get the approval of four Harvard professors for the idea of an undergraduate club devoted to business ventures, Ed did so, getting four of the best-known and respected names on campus (Professors Alfred Chandler, Jesse Markham, Robert Bales, and David McClelland). Eventually, the dean gave in and signed off on the idea. But the delaying tactics had an effect: the club was proposed in February, but it wasn't formally approved until April 28.

It bothered us that while certain other local colleges actually encouraged such entrepreneurial activity as something that provided services for the whole student body, Harvard took an opposite view. We felt that what we were doing was a growing experience, even an intellectually challenging one, and certainly emotionally fulfilling. But the school was discouraging it. If we had wanted to be actors in a university play, that would have been fine. But something like the club, or still later Fuel Tech, was not okay. Or at least it was not encouraged; that bothered us.

Part of the university's problem was that it feared we might do something, using the school name, that would get it sued. But we understood that. We didn't want a club that would try to do business in its own name. We wanted a club that would be a sounding board for ideas. The basic idea at the beginning was, simply, that we had done some small things on campus, and now we wanted to see if we could move off campus and try some bigger ones.

Another reason for forming the club was to use the combined experience of the members. If someone proposed selling ceramic pumpkins, we knew there would be members of the club who could say, "I've done something like that before, and this is what you have to look out for . . ." Or, "I've been involved in retailing and know about inventories and delivery dates and charges on financing." We figured we could pool the talents of the people in the club.

You need ten members to form a club at Harvard, and our first group numbered about twice that; almost all of them were kids we'd handpicked because they had run businesses or been active entrepreneurially. We thought that was a good-sized group to get started with. Our first meeting was a raucous, but productive, affair, complete with expensive beer and big cigars (St. Pauli Girl and El

Productos, Ed's little touch of style). It lasted about two hours and we established the aims and the outline of the organization.

By the beginning of the next school year, it was clear that we were going to have to limit the membership. It all started during registration. Harvard's registration, like that of most schools, probably, is a complicated, complex affair, but it is subdued compared to the competition put on by the various clubs to get new members. We signed up for a booth in the area set aside for all the clubs, not so much because we needed or wanted new members, but because we wanted people to know that we did, finally, exist. Ed manned the booth alone, and although the other clubs had banners and elaborate, costly signs, we had only a table, on which were placed a box of cigars, a yellow legal pad, and a pencil. All we asked for was the names of people who *might* be interested in joining.

We had no trouble attracting students. In fact, that was not a problem at all. They seemed to leave the building where registration was taking place and just stream over to the Entrepreneur's booth. Our problem was that we had been assigned a booth right next to the Friends of the Young Spartacus Society, Harvard's Communist group.

The people who ran the Young Spartacus booth were not at all pleased to see that the university had sanctioned a club for budding capitalists, and they were decidedly displeased to see how many people we were attracting, especially compared to the few who came to their booth. (We got over a hundred signatures during registration, and they got only a dozen, if that many.)

At one point, when one of their group was going out to buy sodas, Ed gave him change and asked him to bring one back for him. The young Communist threw the money at Ed. Later that day Ed asked for a different location. The next day we were next to the dramatic society, a more congenial crew.

Having so many people express interest in joining meant a number of new problems, the main one being that you simply can't discuss ideas very well in a group of a hundred people. Eventually we got it to a workable size. Belonging to the Harvard Entrepreneurs Society has turned out to be a golden opportunity for many of the members because they have finally found others with whom they can share interests and beliefs, and talk about them.

We started the club because we could not find anything like it. We wanted something challenging and exciting and creative, and there was nothing like it on campus. Most of what was on campus was geared toward the pre-professional — pre-law, pre-medicine — and was well accepted. But the pre-business person really didn't have a place on the Harvard campus; it wasn't considered "main line" to be pre-business. There was no *undergraduate* tradition of respect and support for business activities. And yet, ironically, many of the largest contributions from alumni supporters over the years have come from those who have been successful in business.

We like to think we have done something about changing that situation and making the student who is interested in business feel more at home at Harvard.

GAME PLAN   To Form an Undergraduate $ Club

What's Involved

1. Locating individuals who are interested in business.
2. Setting up a forum to encourage and facilitate the flow of ideas.

3.   Encouraging individuals to interact in small groups or one on one, providing an invaluable networking system.

If you are a student, whether at a small liberal arts college off in the woods somewhere, or a multi-thousand-enrollment, big-city school with a concrete campus, we'll bet that you can find several dozen people like yourself who are interested in at least *talking* about making money. If you don't have an organization like ours, then start one! Don't wait for someone else to do it. After all, one of the distinguishing marks of an entrepreneur is his or her ability to get things going.

We have found the theoretical discussions with our fellow entrepreneurs to be almost as valuable as the actual steps we have taken to put those theories, and others, in practice. Also, there is something to be said for making contacts. Even if little comes of it at first, if it's just a bunch of like-minded people sitting around talking to one another and having a good time discussing business, that's not the worst way we can think of to spend an evening. If our experience is any guide, eventually you get down to work — and you enjoy it all.

2

Several
Medium-Sized Deals

The business ventures mentioned in the first part of the book can all be tried, or at least started, by one person. Most of them are naturals for anyone who is going to school. The entrepreneurial examples in this section, however, are different. Each one depends on a good working relationship with several people, though not each one of them has to be an entrepreneurial type, in the "one-man-shop" sense. They all represent more substantial efforts, in both work and challenge, and thus the potential rewards are greater. As with the earlier examples, all of these businesses are run by Harvard students.

There are several examples in this section in which the success of the venture might seem to depend on the special talents of the individual entrepreneur. But, as in the case of Jaime Wolf (the world's youngest Adidas dealer), all these people swear that their accomplishments can be duplicated by enterprising souls without any special talent or skill.

And we agree.

Whatever your interests, you should find something to intrigue you in this section. We feature entertainment, enrichment, partnership, management, jewels, and even a peek into the future.

"Juggles" and Company

Pam Wine is a clown. That's a description, not a put-down. A twenty-one-year-old Economics major from Norwood, Massachusetts — "a bedroom community south of Boston" — Pam started her earliest entrepreneurial venture by taking care of pets while in high school. And then an avocation paid off. Her skill at juggling was to lead, a few years later, into a job as a street clown. When that boomed she started hiring other clowns to work for her. (Finding them was not a problem. As she says, deadpan, "There are a lot of clowns on the street.")

I learned how to juggle while I was in high school, and learning how to juggle is a major part of being a clown. If you can juggle, you can keep children amused. I first got a job working for somebody else, selling balloons by being a clown. And I saw how popular it was. A lot of people would come up to me on the street, approach me, and say, "You're a really good clown; can you do something for my children's birthday party?" I thought, "Hey, this might be a good idea." So I did a couple birthday parties and saw how much money you could make — $30 for an hour's birthday party, and $30 an hour is nothing to sneer at!

Pam soon found that there was even more business than she had anticipated, and she began to audition and hire other clowns. Although she organized the group, Pam did not bother to make it a formal company. As she says, "It was just a bunch of clowns working together." (If you laugh when Pam Wine makes any of these comments, in her matter-of-fact style, she grins and says, "See, I'm a good clown!") But, although she kept the organization quite loose, it got to be rather large. And she was continually surprised at her own success.

This is really easy to do. You just have to have the basic juggling skills, and a few clowning skills. In fact, I didn't really need to be a clown. What I ended up being in the end was more of an administrator or contact person. The clowns who were working for me were doing more clowning than I was. I was just basically talking to people, setting it up, and paying my workers.

What I decided to do, when I got all these clowns together — different people would ask different prices for clowning, depending on the size of the birthday party or the job — was just grant my clowns a specific wage no matter what kind of party they did. Sometimes it would be higher and sometimes it would be lower than the prices I actually received. Most of the time I would make a small profit on them. But that was so they would have a steady wage and know that when they came to me they would get $20 an hour for clowning and I would get about $10 more per hour.

I was called "Juggles the Clown," so I called my outfit "Juggles and Company."

Anyone who might like to set up a clown agency or company should realize first of all that the people you get in a clown company are very idiosyncratic. Because the thing that makes someone become a clown usually makes him or her not your typical, run-of-the-mill person off the street.

Except for money problems, I didn't have too many difficulties dealing with my clowns. But sometimes the job wouldn't go well; clowning jobs don't always go well. If a person had a bad job — say, the kids were really horrible or the parents were ingrates or the clown would have to do a sidewalk sale in 110-degree heat — the clown would come back and say to me, "That was a miserable job. I never want to work here again unless you pay me more," or "How dare you send me out on that job!" But I had no way of knowing ahead of time what the job would turn out to be like, and that's what I'd try to explain.

A lot of my clowns had worked on the street before, but usually just with a hat out on the ground in front of them. Very few of them had ever worked for an organized outfit.

If I were to advise people on running a clown agency, I would warn them to make it a stricter business organization first. I sort of just blundered into it. I saw this money-making opportunity and went ahead with it. But it was all very disorganized and loose, and if I were to do it over again I would set it up properly at the beginning. I would say to myself, "I'm going to get so many clowns, and I'm going to charge so much money, and I'm going to do such-and-such as advertising." Which would be unlike the way I did it, which was just spur of the moment.

But then, I didn't have any capital outlay. I had started during the summer, so by the time school began I had already built up all my connections. People would just call me up, and I'd send out clowns from the school. I had no trouble with the school administration because they didn't know anything about it! All I really needed was my telephone; I didn't have to have a bunch of clowns hanging around the room.

A lot of the people who clowned for me were transient types, people who really didn't have permanent jobs. I had one guy working for me who was thirty-six years old. He'd been in the navy, and he just never really found a place for himself in society. We met while I was clowning, and he said he'd like to do it too, so I said sure. But it was really a total range of people. Mostly older people. Not students, but people in their twenties. Very few of them had aspirations for show business; mostly they were low-level clowns.

Very few of my clowns were extroverts. Most were just the opposite. Many of them were very good with children, but when they would come to me they'd be amazingly shy and introverted. It seemed to be a pattern and was part of the reason my business worked so well; a lot of the introverts couldn't deal with the impact of arranging the clowning dates themselves, and they didn't want to deal with the public. They just wanted to do their clowning and then take their money and go home.

So, the fact that I could be an extrovert in dealing with people and aggressive in arranging dates was really a plus.

I'd never done any business organizing before, but I'd always liked to work for myself. When I was younger I didn't have any specific business, but I was sort of an organizer-type kid. I organized a tree-house club, and when I was in elementary school I organized a school paper. I always was into starting things myself, and being in charge.

During the first summer I was running around Boston constantly, and the money turned out to be very good. Certainly twice as much as I would have made working for a little over the minimum wage. It was definitely profitable.

The hours were strange, a little crazy. Not your typical hours. Especially weekdays. Because people were working during the week and there wasn't much of a call for clowns, except for fairs and occasional sidewalk sales, in which case you could work normal hours. Most times you work evenings and weekends, the hours that most people don't work. But I liked that. It was fine.

When I needed more people, I would try them out, hold clown auditions.

I'd say, "Do your stuff," and "Let me see how you would react to such-and-such a situation." Clowns have different skills — juggling, mime, riding a unicycle — and I would hire different clowns for different things. There are different types of clowns — the clown with the white face, the clown who is a bum — and actually sometimes people would request a specific type. They would say, "I'd like a mime for my party." An adult party. And I could fill those requests because I had a couple of mimes in my "clown stable."

I'd have them do their skills, and then I'd fire some questions at them. Such as "What would you do if a kid hurt himself at a party?" I'd have to teach them specific things like that. Emergency cases. But most of the time it wasn't a problem. Usually they had clowned before, and they knew how to handle themselves.

One thing I would advise anyone interested in setting up a clown business to do would be to look into insurance. I never did, but it worried me at times. I didn't have any problems, but I think I was just lucky.

Once when I was doing a clown party, at a restaurant, with about eighteen little kids, a fire started. There we were, all happily eating hamburgers, and we had to leave. Suddenly all the kids were running out, and I had to keep them from going into the street, which made me pretty nervous because the parents weren't around. But the kids were thrilled.

GAME PLAN   To Provide a Clown Service

A. Market: Children's parties and promotional events for businesses.

  1. Approach: Word of mouth and exposure from performances provided for geometric growth of the business.
  2. Price: The price varied, depending on specifics of the request; $30 per hour was the standard fee.
  3. Timing: This is a year-round business, because most of the activity revolves around birthdays.

B. Competition: Alternate forms of children's entertainment, such as skating rinks and Disney movies, capture part of this service field, but the preference for clowns has staying power. You can't beat a clown for appealing to kids.

C. Goods and Overhead

  1. Materials: A clown's attire and desired performing equipment are necessary.

D. Capital: This venture required no capital, just talent.

  1. Cash flow: The clown-for-cash approach provides for immediate cash flow.

E. Risk

  1. Financial: With no start-up capital and immediate payment for service, the risk is nil.
  2. Hidden Dangers: Possible liability in the event a child becomes sick or injured.

3. Word of Caution: Insurance is a necessity for anyone considering operating such a service.

F. Time Commitment: This can easily be done part time and at flexible hours.

G. What's Involved
   1. Finding clowns who want to work.
   2. Arranging engagements for them.
   3. Laughing all the way to the bank.

Like so many good business people, or people who take to business matters rather naturally, Pam Wine makes the clown business sound a little easier than it is. One thing anyone who might like to start a similar business should keep in mind is that there is a fair amount of detail work involved, and the owner-operator of such a venture should be a good organizer. Also, and this is why we put "Juggles" in the "Medium" section, a business like this has the potential to grow into a fairly good-sized operation, with the owner doing little more than administrative duties. Pam says that she did not spend much time or money on advertising, but that was her choice, since she had as much business as she wanted. Someone else (someone with more clowns) might want to operate on a larger scale, and the potential is certainly there. We feel this is an excellent kind of business for an entrepreneur who wants to proceed a step at a time. Indeed, like Pam, you can start as a solo act and graduate to a whole "stable" of clowns.

The Brown Family Day Camp

Richard Brown,* from Santa Fe, New Mexico, is one of eight children. The twenty-one-year-old junior, a Fine

* Not his real name

Arts major with a concentration in Art History, definitely believes in keeping it all in the family. He and his sisters and brothers have created a mini–family empire in the suburban wilds of Santa Fe.

At a very early age, Richard noticed that his older sisters, back from college, were dissatisfied with having only the choice of working "junk jobs at McDonald's for an hourly wage." Six years ago, when he was not even halfway through high school, Richard Brown saw an article in a newspaper that mentioned Santa Fe's critical need for *summer* day camps. He and his two older sisters decided to go into that business. They have not stopped since.

We decided to start our own summer day camp, using the property behind our house, which was on about a half acre, and which had a swimming pool. We thought we would start and just see what happened. We would teach a lot of special interests, like swimming and other sports and arts and crafts, things like that.

At first it was pretty depressing. We worked really hard. And we made $400 apiece for the whole summer. But by last year we were doing really well; we signed up forty kids. Every week. We had waiting lists. The three original people, my two sisters and I, made $4,100 apiece. Our two other sisters and another brother made a little bit less, because they weren't working the same hours.

For me, one of the main points of business is sharing the wealth — we have had to hire outside people too — really splitting it up. We all work five-hour days, twenty hours a week, four days a week, with Fridays off. That's eight twenty-hour weeks. So we made that amount of money in 160 hours — the number of hours the camp is open. But the aides arrive at eight and the kids leave at three, so someone is really there from eight to six. But the idea of splitting really gives everybody a fair share — and it keeps people on their toes. You can't let counselors who are dealing with kids get bored. When they're making $10 or $20 an hour, they'll stay awake.

We've grown from twelve campers the first summer to about forty last summer. But it really varies. They sign up by the week; some weeks there might be eight and other weeks maybe twenty-two. So every week we made a different amount of money.

We had to pay attention to the requirements. New Mexico has three kinds of licenses — day-care center, day camp, and nursery (which can be just about anything, and basically is baby-sitting). The first year we had a nursery license. For the next license, the day-*care* license, I checked with an attorney first. We had to get liability insurance, and we really had to study up on all of that. But we got lucky the very first year because the guy we talked to at the insurance company worked hard for us and gave us a really good deal — for $450 a summer we get half a million dollars' worth of liability insurance. And all that's not that difficult, especially because we've never had an accident. But we do have a pool, so we have to be careful, we really patrol the pool.

Overall, we never have more than a one-to-eight ratio, one teacher for every eight kids. The kids pay a lot — $40 a week, which is $10 a day or $2.00 an hour.

I have some definite warnings for anyone who might like to try to run a day camp. The rules for licensing day camps are changing in my state, and everyone should check out the *latest* rules in their own localities. Be extremely careful in hiring your help. A recent case represented the worst thing that could happen — a guy who ran a day-camp center was brought up on twenty or twenty-one counts of sexual harassment of children. Pay strict attention to sanitation regulations. A spot inspection of three licensed pools turned up algae growing on the walls, and the camps were closed down.

We've never had such problems, but even so, we may have to get more insurance this year.

To do what we did doesn't take all that much start-up money, but it takes a *lot* to keep operating. You have to think, for example, about the impact on the neighborhood. Our neighbors were not especially pleased about the idea. You have to realize that when you are running a backyard business, you may be blamed for anything that goes wrong. It's another hassle to deal with.

Another thing that's especially important is accounting. You ought at least to read a book about it. Initially, you have a lot of cash and checks coming in, a stack of checks at the beginning of the week. Forty kids times forty bucks, that's sixteen hundred bucks. If you don't have a real set plan as to what to do with your money ahead of time — how it's going to be split up and budgeted — you can have a lot of trouble. And, of course, there are taxes.

Families are really a good thing. I never really worked for or with anybody but my family, my whole life. I wake up, and I'm at work. I get breakfast free. I don't have to drive anywhere. And if I want to skip a day, it's no problem going in to straighten it out.

Also, it keeps you on your toes, because not only are you responsible for your own wages, but your family is counting on you. I think that people who are in partnerships should be really good friends, or at least really understand one another. I'm told that's not the standard business advice, but it's been my experience.

I've been involved in other ventures, also with the family. About four years ago, my brother Joe, who is now seventeen and a junior in high school, asked me to help him get a business going, building and selling playground equipment and playhouses for families. He only asked me because he couldn't drive. So I said, yeah, sure, and asked him if he had any jobs, and he did!

So we started designing a few things, and got a few jobs. One woman paid us $400 for a playground set. That worked well; we put up another one that same summer, and then the next year we incorporated. There was only one other guy in Santa Fe doing custom work — in a city of 49,000. We've been doing all right, and this summer we should surpass the day-care money — which for me last year was about $4,100 — for sure. We didn't make as much last year because we bought a pickup truck and tools and a ladder. This summer we'll have six people working full time for us.

What we're trying to do now is to put together a kit for the playground equipment. I really enjoy the designing, and I've been doing some of that here at school. We have only one more stage to go, copyrighting our plans. Then we can offer them for sale just like a kit for, say, building a garage.

Based on his various business experiences, Richard Brown has formed certain general observations that we feel are worth passing on to the reader. The first is important to younger entrepreneurs.

Age makes a lot of difference in dealing with customers. It gets easier the older you get. Say you're talking to someone on the phone and he wants you to come out and look at a site — he's interested and as nice as can be, but when you show up and he sees how young you are, he changes entirely. My seventeen-year-old brother is probably the most competent of us all. He's really sharp, he knows what's going on, and he knows our products, because he *builds* our stuff. But when he shows up, people who really don't know anything start to push him around and tell him what to do. They assume that a kid is going to do a lousy job.

The first few times that happened, we just got mad, and frustrated, and ended up with really bad experiences. We wanted to get out of there as soon as we could. There are laws that say you can keep customers thirty feet away while you're working, but a lot of our business is by word of mouth. We always try our best to be as nice as possible, but some people make it almost impossible.

The best way to handle it is to be prepared. Sometimes we precut our wood the night before in our garage, even if we have to stay up until two or three in the morning, so that when we show up we'll only be there a few hours. Then the customers see the thing going right up, which usually impresses them so much that they shut up.

If customers insist on alterations to your plans that you feel may make the finished product dangerous, have them sign a form relieving you of responsibility. That way you protect yourself from being sued if a child, or anyone, gets hurt.

As for other ventures, this summer Joe and I are going to start a pool-cleaning business. My brother has a lot of friends in his class who are really good, sharp guys. Instead of letting them sit around all summer, we're going to get them to go to work for us. We may even get another truck.

It seems to me that with the economy the way it is, there are still three things that are going to make money. One is anything having to do with saving energy; another is the type of object that people want no matter what, like certain items of clothing or games; and the third is services.

In regard to services, if you can prove to people that you can do a job better than your competitors, or better, cheaper, quicker, and more efficiently than they can do it themselves, they're always going to hire you. Especially if you can convince them that you can do it cheaper.

It excites me, if that's the right word, when I see something being done the wrong way. I know I can do it better and cheaper — everything from street construction to just the way doors work. Don't you ever go into an office and see things that are just not the way they should be? Because of that, I think services are going to do well in the future.

This summer will be a good indicator of how good some of my ideas are, because we're going to try a whole lot of things. For example, we're going to have a hauling business. The garbage men won't take certain things — tree limbs, for instance — but you can hire city of Santa Fe employees to do it for a fee. They charge $20 flat for the first hour and, I think, another $20 for the second. Well, it doesn't cost $40 to haul that stuff away!

We experimented last summer for three weeks, using our truck. We advertised a $25 flat rate. We put in another phone line, and got three guys to work for us. We even got the people from the city to refer us! They didn't want to do that kind of job! It worked very well for us.

I've been involved in a few entrepreneurial ventures at school, but I work so hard during the summers that when I get back to classes I concentrate on my studies.

Richard Brown's attitude about separating college and business stems from his father's influence. Mr. Brown, a law professor and tax-law expert, worked so hard during his own school days that he wanted his kids to have an easier life. In keeping with that philosophy, when he taught at a law school in New York City one summer, he brought Richard, then about to enter his senior year of high school, along and told him not to work but to learn and enjoy the city. Richard ended up working, for nothing, with some friends who ran a soup kitchen in the Bowery.

GAME PLAN **Day Camp: To Provide Recreational Activities For Children Five to Nine Years Old**

A. Market: A critical need for summer day camps in the Santa Fe area.

1. Approach: To provide the market with the service defined as "needed."
2. Price: $40 a week per child for a total of twenty hours per week of service.
3. Timing: Summertime.

B. Competition: Existing summer day camps did not meet the market demand, but potential expansion of existing camps or the opening of new summer camps could affect the marketability of the Browns' camp.

C. Goods and Overhead

1. Equipment: Swimming pool.
2. Facilities: Recreational area for sports and arts and crafts.

D. Capital: The equipment and facilities necessary to operate and open the camp required no capital outlay.
   1. Cash flow: The weekly fee for the service eliminated potential cash-flow problems.
E. Regulations: Licenses to operate such a camp vary from state to state.
F. Risk
   1. Financial: This camp has little to nothing at risk.
   2. Hidden Danger: The potential for lawsuits necessitates liability insurance.
G. Time Commitment: Even though one's hours may be flexible, the effort and time required are demanding.
H. What's Involved
   1. Obtaining access to the necessary equipment and facilities to operate a summer camp.
   2. Complying with state and local regulations.
   3. Obtaining liability insurance.
   4. Setting up an accounting system.
   5. Providing recreation and instruction for the children.

Clearly, Richard Brown is a guy with a lot of ideas. His family's summer-day-camp business is one that many readers could try. The Browns happened to have a pool, which gave them an advantage, but a pool is not necessary for this type of business. In fact, some people would prefer not to have the responsibility that goes with being in charge of other people's children in or near a swimming pool. Note that the Browns ran the business — which brought in over $1,500 during good weeks — with no more than five or six "employees" at peak times. A smaller group of individuals could start such a business on a smaller scale, and experiment to see if the Browns' one counselor for every eight children is the best ratio.

It probably should go without saying, but not everyone is suited for working with children, so be very careful when you select partners or employees. On the other hand, working with kids can often be far preferable to working with adults!

GAME PLAN **Playground Sets: To Build Customized Playground Sets**

A. Market: Residents of the city of Santa Fe (Population: 49,000).

   1. Approach: Phase 1: To expand service by word of mouth.
Phase 2: To wholesale a do-it-yourself kit to building-supply stores for resale.

   2. Pricing: Varies, depending on design, but begins at $250.

   3. Timing: Year round.

B. Competition: One other competitor in Santa Fe.

C. Goods and Overhead

   1. Materials: Lumber, nails, and other durable building goods.

   2. Equipment: Truck, ladder, and carpenter's tools.

D. Capital

   1. Up-front capital needed to purchase equipment, materials, and insurance, and for legal fees.

   2. Cash flow: Payments for service and materials can be arranged so as to minimize cash-flow difficulties.

E. Regulations: There may be building codes that bear on the construction of the playground, so state and local authorities should be informed.

F. Risk

    1. Financial: The equipment and materials necessary for this operation are "liquidable," minimizing the financial risk.

    2. Hidden Dangers: Liability for faulty construction and/or design features that may cause harm to a user.

G. Time Commitment: This venture requires manual labor, so the hours vary depending on consumer demand.

H. What's Involved

    1. Designing a playground set.

    2. Constructing the set.

This is an example of a business that is based on — as was the summer-day-care camp — recognizing and taking advantage of a need in your area. Before starting an operation like building customized playground equipment, you should make a careful study of the market and the competition. For example, if your neighborhood has plenty of parks that are filled with free equipment, you might have trouble selling this type of service. But if not, just the opposite could be true. Also, before going ahead compare the prices of what is available locally (the ready-made sets) with what you will have to charge for your customized sets. Just as you don't want to undercharge, you also don't want to price yourself out of the market. Finally, don't be put off by what might strike you as the need for sophisticated carpentry skills. The ability required is really rather basic. You might consider starting this kind of a business on a trial basis, figuring out your profit — on a per-hour scale — fairly soon. You want to make sure you are spending your time efficiently.

A Partnership within a Partnership

Part of the incentive in doing things like this
is the *fun*. Because at times you feel like
you're playing a really big game. You know
you're playing for a large stake! It's not like
you're playing Monopoly and can say you're
tired and you quit.

— Chip Hawk

Chip Hawk, twenty, a Government and History major
from Atlanta, and Dave Belluck, also twenty and an
Economics major from Roslyn Heights, New York, are
both juniors. Unlike the majority of people mentioned in
the book, they were looking for something they could
work on together, something they could use as a growth
experience, a kind of off-campus learning tool.

As things turned out, they may have found exactly
what they were looking for.

DAVE: We're both members of the Harvard Entrepreneurs
club. We've been sitting in on meetings and have heard
different ideas thrown out on the floor, and we've been
looking to start a company or a business or to market a
specific product. We recently heard about an inventor
who was looking for someone to market his product. The
inventor liked the idea of having a couple of students
work on it. He has an M.B.A. from Harvard, and he was
involved in some business deals when he was in college.

CHIP: Apparently, the inventor has been working on it for
about four or five years, but hasn't had the time to market it. He read the article about the club in the *New York
Times* and called. We met him, and here we are.

DAVE: We probably should mention the apprehension we
went through. I remember when the product was first
described to us. It's a silent phone, a silent communica-

tion device. It's in two pieces — one to go on a secretary's desk, and the other on an executive's desk. When the executive gets a phone call, the secretary can answer it; then, without putting the caller on hold or without interrupting the executive, she can type on a little keyboard, and a message appears on a screen on the executive's desk. Because it's a silent message, it doesn't interrupt him if he's in conference or on another call, and he can reply by punching eight or nine different buttons, signaling different responses.

The inventor has already built the first model, the prototype. He also has a patent on the software aspect of it. We wondered whether it could be sold to another company as part of a larger package, a computer package. Or should it be sold to stores, and if so, how difficult would it be to market?

Those were some of the things we were apprehensive about. I had been skeptical about trying to sell such a product in the kind of economy we're in right now. But after we met with the inventor and saw the machine, we no longer felt that way and were ready to go ahead.

CHIP: Mitch Gould, the inventor, is the president of a company that has nothing to do with his invention, so he really needed somebody to help him take it the rest of the way. Basically, Dave and I will be doing all the day-to-day operations of the company.

We're getting the financing for the company, and we'll take care of the manufacturing end and the marketing. The whole thing.

DAVE: We're sketching a business plan, which is very important, even though at the beginning we have to put down arbitrary time periods. We just figured that two months for this stage and two months for that stage made sense. When we actually sat down with Mitch we found ourselves having to explain each step, and we realized that, because the whole process was so new to us, we were actually learning as we went along. Some of the Statistics courses I've studied came in handy in doing the market survey, but basically we're just using common sense.

CHIP: There are a lot of people around here we can go to for advice. Some of them are very good. We got a lot of help from some graduate students, economics majors who have operated businesses of their own or are about to start them.

DAVE: The two who have helped us most are in the Law School, and they've been more than happy to sit down with us and discuss our ideas and what we should be aware of. Because we really had no idea — or at least I didn't — of what we were getting into. For example, even though Mitch has had a patent on this device for five years, and has been able to fight off other inventors who tried to copy it, we found out we will still have to do a patent search to find out how tight his piece of paper is.

Having hashed and rehashed the market plan, we now have set ideas about how much money will be needed and when, and we have set periods for its various uses. Which is something very important to a business that's just starting out.

CHIP: The negotiation process itself has been very much a learning experience. We drew up our business plan, and had to justify each stage and step of it to him. We've had two meetings where we've sat down and given him our ideas and plans and he's come up with his reservations, ideas, and innovations. Just working with him at those two meetings I've probably learned more about the working of the business world than I would have in months on my own.

DAVE: In addition to his M.B.A., Mitch has a law degree and has worked as a lawyer, but right now, while he is running someone else's business, he doesn't have any real time to devote to this. So he's drawing up the incorporation papers — which we will then have our own lawyers look at — and it will be a fifty-fifty deal. We're to take care of the day-to-day running of the company, and he (as a member of the board of directors) will consult on major decisions. We are not being paid now, but after the papers are signed we will all decide on the compensation involved.

We're going to raise the capital in intervals. We've decided how much we're going to need over the next eighteen months. The first few thousand dollars will go for the patent search, the incorporation fee, and our lawyers' fees, unless we have to pay for that ourselves. The next money will go for the prototype; we're going to be searching for a manufacturer to produce this cheaply. Then we'll be having prototypes made, and put them in offices to get some feedback from executives.

We may also decide to do some more engineering on it because, right now, the two units are connected by a wire. We think $30,000 or $35,000 ought to be enough to design it so it's not connected by a wire, which I think is a necessity if we are going to be successful.

Mitch has been very helpful, especially in asking us questions about why we are proposing to do certain things certain ways.

CHIP: Right now we're trying to get funding, and we're talking with investors. It's a lot of give-and-take because they're trying to get as much equity in our company as they can for their money and we're trying to keep as much as we can.

DAVE: We've only been working on this project for about two months, but we've already done quite a bit. We thought about it for a while, then made some preliminary calls, to see if there was any demand for it. And we've gotten positive feedback from everyone we've run the invention by, including a couple of retail chains that sell office equipment. The computer companies with which we've discussed the product think it would be helpful in offices. So in no sense are we going into this blindly.

As far as the amount of time we put into it, that varies. It has usually been just going from one minicrisis to another. Like the time Chip saw an ad in the *Wall Street Journal* for a product that looked exactly like ours. It was on a morning we were scheduled to have one of our final meetings with Mitch about our agreement. We were in shock. We had to wait fifteen minutes before we could see him, and we had the ad with us. We said to each other, "This meeting sure isn't going to go the way he thinks it is, and we sure aren't going to be our usual optimistic and enthusiastic selves." But when we saw him he wasn't upset at all. He already knew about the product, and patiently explained to us that it did something quite different.

But it's a day-to-day thing. We spend quite a few hours a few days in a row and then we won't get anything in the mail for a week. But even when we have the contract, we won't work full time right away.

The first couple of months are going to be the most important. Because if we can't find a manufacturer who can make it a lot more cheaply than it is being made now, it is probably not going to be a viable product. So we'll just have to see. But that's why it's important how our agreement is drawn — so that if we have to get out after the first two months we can.

CHIP: This kind of arrangement may seem unusual, but it isn't when you're dealing with inventors. You often have to put some of your own money into a company too, though we haven't had to do that with Mitch. Some deals with inventors give the entrepreneurs the option to buy out the inventor eventually. Many, maybe even most, inventors are not also business-oriented, but we're fortunate that Mitch has business experience. He's not at all a "flaky inventor."

DAVE: Not at all. I was very impressed when we met him. Besides, in a year's time, if this project is developing well, he will devote more time to it, somehow.

This whole thing is really quite different from what most of the other entrepreneurs are doing because we are doing the whole thing, but with someone else's initial idea or product. We're finding the whole deal to be a great learning experience.

My goal is to keep learning. If it makes it, great. But if it doesn't, all I'm risking is a time commitment that basically, at the moment, I can afford to risk. And it's an awful lot of fun!

CHIP: There are all sorts of other benefits that will continue even if the company doesn't go on to make all kinds of money. For example, I went to interview for a summer job, and the guy asked me about my interests and what kind of projects I was involved in, and I told him about this. He was so impressed, he didn't even bother to interview anyone else and gave me the job right away. A lot of businessmen are pleased to see kids who will take a chance on something like this and show some initiative. The experience allows you to deal with an adult in the business community on a much more competent level.

To be very honest, what we're doing doesn't take a great deal of intelligence. What it takes is a great deal of running around, and a great deal of telephoning. I keep the Yellow Pages right next to my bed.

GAME PLAN   To Manufacture and Market a Silent Interoffice Communicator

A. Market: Locations where a central operator receives incoming calls, then directs them to the appropriate persons; for example, secretaries who answer the phone for their bosses.

　　1. Approach: Either through licensing, direct sales, wholesale, or any combination of the above.

　　2. Price: This will vary greatly, depending on approach used, but it should run around $200.

　　3. Timing: Once the manufacturing and design aspect have been completed, the market penetration of this novel and practical product should be immediate.

B. Competition: This product is patented, so the competition is nonexistent. Also, existing technology that provides similar functions, such as the hold key on phones or intercoms, fare poorly in comparison.

C. Goods and Overhead

   1. Materials: Key to this venture's success is the ability to secure low-cost materials, because a low-cost end product will appeal to a wider market.

D. Capital: Over $50,000 will be needed before quantity manufacturing can begin.

E. Risk

   1. Financial: Since the initial capital provides funds for services and materials which, in the event the product never reaches market, will not generate a return on investsment, the investors will have "at least" a tax loss.

F. Time Commitment: This venture involves continued hustle and persistence and, at moments of heightened activity or "crises," total time commitment.

G. What's Involved

   1. Finding a new, slightly imperfect invention.
   2. Solving engineering problems.
   3. Figuring out the cost benefit of the solution; in other words, there's no point in spending $1,000 to save $10.
   4. Implementing a means of production.
   5. Marketing the finished product.

The intriguing thing about this venture is that it indicates how much one can find out about business on a learn-as-you-go basis, without spending any money. (Of course, neither Chip nor Dave has *made* any money yet, but they knew that's how it would be going in.) Of vital importance in such a deal is to have points charted along the way, as they have done, where you can pull out. This is particularly important for arrangements in which those who do the work of marketing have no capital of their own invested and thus are able to offer only their effort and enthusiasm.

The key to success in such a venture is to find both a product you can sell with sincerity and people with whom you can work compatibly. Chip and Dave both realize that if their effort does not work out, it will not be because they weren't given a chance to prove what they can do. And that, on the other hand, accounts in large part for their enthusiasm.

Chip and Dave were approached through the club, but readers may want to try direct advertising — in newspapers, magazines, and trade journals — as a way of finding inventors or manufacturers who need help. People who cannot afford to pay you initially are more apt to be generous with stock arrangements.

Entrepreneurs-in-Waiting

The three people we want you to meet next are a little different. In fact, you may think they don't actually belong in a book about entrepreneurs because they all work for someone else — and our original definition of an entrepreneur is someone who works for himself or herself. But we feel these three people are special because even though they work for someone else for a set wage (plus a bonus) and are supposed to work set hours, they are *managers*. The skills they bring to these management tasks are definitely those of the entrepreneur.

A private, off-campus company known as the HSA, short for Harvard Student Agencies, performs many of the basic tasks that most schools do themselves, including such things as the linen service, custodial service, catering, and a variety of others. There are eleven different agencies or divisions of HSA, each run by a Harvard student.

Competition for these positions is stiff. The winners

are supposed to show the largest "profit" possible, which is a way of encouraging and rewarding individualism, not discouraging it. We are including these three HSA managers because we realize that not everyone who reads this book is free to take the entrepreneurial plunge. Some of you know that because of family or school obligations (or both) you have to work for someone else for a while. But we want you to see that you can do it in a way that develops your entrepreneurial skills.

Also, we want to suggest that if your school does not have an organization like the Student Agencies, you might consider starting one. A lot of schools would probably like to get out of the linen business, for example, if they could find someone responsible to take it over. You might find yourself an excellent entrepreneurial opportunity.

Bryan Hunter. Bryan Hunter, a twenty-year-old junior from Nyack, New York, is a Government major. His main interest is in international finance and banking, which he may use in the future in his native Jamaica.

HSA is a nonprofit, student-run corporation. There is a full-time staff — a business manager, an operations manager, and a general manager who is in charge of the daily operations of the company. Some students serve on the board of directors; the president of the corporation is a student. I am the manager of the agency called the Harvard Distribution Services. We offer such services as door-to-door distribution of papers, leafletting, postering on campus, and what I'm working on now — developing a courier service for the Cambridge and Boston area.

I have an assistant manager and a director of marketing, because much of our business is based on door-to-door distribution of flyers for profit-making firms. For our courier service we will probably have to expand our full-time staff to include some more marketing agents and a dispatcher. We will probably also have to buy more vehicles. We have a van now, but we have been concentrating on foot couriers and public transportation or bikes, as our main service between Cambridge and Boston and within Cambridge and Boston.

My employee pool right now consists of sixty students. Some do the weekly door-to-door and some subcontracted courier work that we do for Harvard. But mostly we just call up these people when we have jobs for them, rather than having specified hours of work.

Mine is supposed to be a fifteen-hour-a-week job, but at times it takes me as much as thirty hours. Writing reports in the office and organizing the courier service takes a lot of time.

This job is particularly good for me because I plan to enter the Business School, and I'm getting managerial experience, which is a prerequisite for admission. In initiating the courier service I've gotten entrepreneurial experience because it's just like starting a small business. I've had to deal with the Massachusetts Department of Public Utilities in getting the license, and that in itself is an experience.

Kyle Kirkland. Sophomore Economics major Kyle Kirkland, formerly a big fish in the little pond of Brewer, Maine, has a history of what amounted to entrepreneurial work for a boss who gave him fairly free rein, and a lot of authority and responsibility. While in high school, he worked in a large supermarket, where he convinced his boss, the store owner, to let him be his "eyes and ears" for the small problems and opportunities the owner might otherwise miss. In one year, Kyle's suggestions and promotions accounted for $16,000 in increased revenue.

Kyle runs the Freshman Union, a huge hall where all the freshmen eat and many of them relax. In this age of video games and snack food, concessions there are a gold mine. (Yes, Virginia, there is a Pac-Man at Harvard.)

Right after I came to school here I started working for the dorm crews, cleaning, and worked through the ranks a bit there. I found I had more free time than I thought I would — and I like to spend money — so one day when I was walking through HSA I noticed this job being advertised. It was "assistant manager for distribution," and I thought, "Hey, I might go for that." So I applied, not really expecting to get it because I was a freshman, and went through the interview process and everything, and they ended up giving it to me! I think that's when I really started rolling.

You can get an awful lot of very valuable experience from HSA. There are eleven managerial positions, and I would define the managers of the agencies as entrepreneurs. HSA employs 1,400 people throughout the year.

The managers can kind of run their own businesses, do their own thing. You get a lot of good managerial experience and a chance to act on your own. A couple of professional staff help you out so you don't go overboard and do anything crazy.

After a year and two months I got a little bored but I wanted to stay within HSA, with Distribution, so I moved over to the Freshman Union. Now I run it. I was also elected to the board of directors of HSA.

But, between the time I was working as assistant manager for Distribution and going to the Freshman Union, I got involved in something else. A friend of mine — my manager's roommate — who was president of the Harvard *Independent* newspaper, contacted me, and he told me that they had a phototypesetting piece of equipment that they were using only three days a week. "What can you do for us? Is there any way you can make some money? We're thinking about doing some résumés and posters. Can you help us out?"

Another friend had started doing it, but he dropped out after two weeks; I stuck with it, and we ended up doing a résumé business through the Business School. The Harvard Business School has an office where first- and second-year students bring in résumés to be done; they would send them over to us, we'd typeset them, send them back, and get the money for them.

My job was pretty much just to *establish* that connection. We hadn't been doing that up to that point so we had to make contacts at the B School, finding out names of people to see, and such.

They already had a concession, but their typesetters were very sensitive, and they weren't really that good. Plus we were pretty much on campus, and I was a little more flexible than they were, I think.

I knew some people from HSA who could type, so I scrounged them up. It was a beautiful piece of phototypesetting equipment. So we just started going to it.

At first we were doing only ten résumés a week. We were doing a terrible job. But eventually we were doing eighty to a hundred a week. And we were charging $12 to $15 a résumé.

We also ended up doing phototypesetting for a number of magazines around Harvard — the *International Review*, the *Advocate*, and a new newspaper called the *Salient*. It really got to be quite a business.

Eventually, I was making $300 or $400 a week, which for a job that was supposed to be part time, was *nice*. That was a good experience.

Then I took over the Freshman Union. There's a rec room downstairs with video games and a wide-screen TV, and we show videotapes. We run a candy stand–variety store in the building too. The second floor contains all kinds of studios — a dance studio, study rooms, and parlors for meetings and things like that. I'm in charge of that whole building. The university owns it, and HSA has contracted to run it. We do custodial, maintaining the whole building, except for structural problems. With attendants on each level, we have about sixty or seventy people there. We do very well. It's *the* most profitable agency.

That's probably been my best experience here. By the strictest definition of entrepreneur — starting your own business — no, that doesn't fit me because I just kind of walked into it. I think that in two months we've done a *lot* over there, brought in things that other people hadn't even thought of. But when I think of entrepreneur, I think of someone who generates business, whether brand-new or innovative.

We've expanded. We've doubled our product line in the variety store. We have everything you could possibly imagine for students, plus snack foods — sodas, candies — and whatever they want, like T-shirts.

Last year we put in, with HSA money, of course, video machines downstairs. The video machines are making a significant amount of money. The craze has come out on campuses everywhere. We have three pool tables down there, and we just put in a wide-screen TV. The building is still kind of bleak, and we're trying to do more with it. Since I've been there, I've purchased a video cassette recorder, and we show free movies every weekend. We're starting to draw a big crowd. And I just happen to carry food downstairs now.

When I signed my contract with HSA to manage the Union, I had to set up a budget. I went over it with the accountant. I wanted a lot of money for advertising; I asked the HSA to be flexible on purchases I wanted to make. I will probably exceed that budget, and for the most part they want me to. One of my feelings is that you can't really make money unless you spend money.

I really enjoy my job because I'm starting to see a lot of the results of my labor. Also, it kind of lets you be a big shot a little bit.

Next year, based on this year's profits, I'm budgeted to go into six figures. I can spend that much money. If I go over a certain profit figure I get a bonus.

As to the extent of entrepreneurial activity at Harvard, I'm more and more surprised at how much of it there is. You don't hear about a lot of stuff because people are sort of hush-hush, but I think there's even more under-ground entrepreneurial activity than people think.

Brian Mullaney. Brian Mullaney's background list of occupations reads as if it came from the dust jacket of a first novel. He has been a piano player in nightclubs and bars, an artist, and a few years ago he dropped out of Harvard for two years. The twenty-three-year-old Economics major is from Westport, Massachusetts, and shortly after his return to Harvard he turned his artistic talents to a new and different use — *founding* a brand-new HSA agency.

I got into this — starting HSA's Advertising Service — basically because I was an advertising artist, a cartoonist. I did a lot of work in that line. About a year ago I applied for a job with Harvard Student Agencies as an artist. They really didn't have a department, just a couple of people who could draw posters and paste up letters. That was the extent of it.

I started doing a lot of the work, and I really liked it. Flyers and little dinky ads. It was a primitive operation, and for a corporation (HSA) that has sales of $1.5 million, it was pretty poor.

But I learned more about it, I took some art courses from an artist in Boston, and learned how to typeset. Harvard doesn't offer courses like that. Too commercial.

We began to put out some good pieces, and at the end of the summer, I quit my other job as a loan collector and decided to go with it full time. I was taking a big pay cut — I was making $6.50 an hour as a loan collector and only $4.00 as an artist, but I got the idea to develop it into an agency, to market our services and take on outside clients. And to produce ads, campaigns, brochures, and everything an ad agency would do.

We started it in the fall as HSA Advertising. It's been an incredible learning experience. No one told me how to do it; I just do it and make mistakes and learn by going back and doing it again.

We hired a bunch of students and tried to train them, but that was hard because they're Harvard students. They're not geared for sales or marketing anything commercially; they're theoretical and have taken courses in the history of art. They know *that*, rather than how to put out a good ad.

Now it's developed fairly well. Our sales are up to about $6,000 or $7,000 a month. The first four months we lost about $1,500, and had gross sales of about $7,000. Now it's growing by bounds and leaps. We haven't done any advertising for ourselves, but we have a lot of major companies coming after us for work. Our profits, of course, belong to HSA.

Now we have four artists, two office people, and me. I work about thirty to forty hours a week, at odd times.

In effect I've founded and am running a business, which I had never done before. I've had a lot of work experience because I dropped out of school and worked for two years. I moved to Los Angeles and worked for several banks in Beverly Hills. Then I came back here and worked for a bank as a loan collector, but I never worked in the field.

The reason I was driven into what became Harvard Advertising Services wasn't the desire to run my own business, but to do what I like, as long as it is creative. It's like when I was a piano player in bars; I'd never had piano lessons, never even had a teacher. I did it on my own. I don't get kicks from being my own boss, though that's fine, but I just like to do what I want to do.

It's also important to me to break out of the mold. Especially here at Harvard, where you're surrounded by a lot of clones. Investment-banker types.

I also do a lot of free-lance work, design and creative, rather than art work. I like the art work and I'm okay at it, but I've never taken any design courses, or pursued it enough. So I concentrate on the creative marketing strategy.

Although Harvard Student Agencies is not entrepreneurial by nature, it does provide employment opportunities for students and a creative, managerial role for the manager of each agency.

Bryan Hunter. Bryan manages the Distribution division, which provides delivery of newspapers, leaflets, notices, and posts posters. He initiated the HSA courier system, which has given him much entrepreneurial experience. He spends approximately fifteen to thirty hours each week supervising his sixty employees.

Kyle Kirkland. Kyle has transformed the Union, the freshman dining facility, into an unofficial student center. He has introduced video games, free movies, and a variety store, which keep his sixty employees busy. Kyle's opportunistic style led him to create a résumé typesetting service, making use of machine downtime. He ended up making almost $50 an hour!

Brian Mullaney. Now that outside companies are knocking down his door, Brian worries that his Advertising Division may not be able to handle all the work. But Brian loves the growing pains. He now employs four artists and two office assistants.

Presenting the One and Only . . . Tahiti Ted!

It took Edward Barton Teele seven years to become a Harvard senior, but the delay was not caused by lack of ambition or the ability to work hard. Ted, now a twenty-four-year-old senior (Social Theory major) entered Harvard in the fall of 1975, but, after one year, left to travel. And travel he did, at one point racing a friend in a hitchhiking competition across the United States and then the world.

One of the stops he enjoyed most was in the South Seas, where he picked up several items that would stay with him — his nickname, a tattoo, and his jewelry business. Fascinated by the beautiful and delicate island jewelry, Ted eventually set up shop selling it on top of a mountain site on the Caribbean island of Saint Thomas, where he did very well.

Later, back in the States, he sold jewelry during the summers — in his hometown of Washington, D.C. — from four different locations. A 1979 *Washington Post* article referred to him as "Midas on the Mall." He also opened a branch in Harvard Square (a "branch" meaning a sidewalk vendor's table), but his energy led him into several other pursuits. He started a dancing school, "Jitterbug a Specialty," and played a lot of house sports, especially Frisbee. In his last few months at Harvard, he was also trying to find the time to write a book urging the abolition of nuclear warfare and weaponry.

There is only one Tahiti Ted.

I didn't get involved in entrepreneurial things as a young person, but I tend to try to do things for myself, in general, and so the jewelry business was the way I paid for my college.

I took three years off. I started in college in 1975; the next year I went to the South Pacific and traveled all over the Pacific. My tattoo, which is a bracelet of boars' tusks, is from Samoa.

I love Harvard. I think it's a wonderful place. But I just thought, after my first year, that I had to travel. My friend David Swetzoff and I decided to try to go around the world. I didn't think about it a great deal, but I just knew that my whole life would be better if I did it. It has turned out to be true, because travel enriched me tremendously. I've been pretty lucky. I believe that even if you do things for yourself, luck plays a tremendous part.

I always knew I would come back to school. Perhaps I was trying to find myself, and perhaps I did, to a certain degree; I mean, it's a never-ending process of coming to find yourself, but going away really helped me in that respect because I had to explain what America was like to people in New Zealand and Australia and Fuji. Places like that. I had to think about what it is to be a student and why I'm at school. Many people may know already, and not have to do that, but for me it was very helpful. Having taken so much time off from school, right now I'm really enjoying it. It's a thrill.

I brought the jewelry back the first time, and I've been having it shipped in ever since. It's a great business, it gives me a lot of freedom, and it's paid my way in college. I sold $94,000 worth of jewelry in 1980, mostly in Saint

Thomas, despite having to pay $3,500 a month for rent. That was the only year I worked full time, all year.

A lot of people ask me whether they should go into the jewelry business, but I don't always recommend it. I don't think there's any great virtue in business. The only great advantage of being a good businessman like I am is being able to make money, but other than that it's not an end in itself. I love people, and I guess that's one reason I'm good at it. But you have to have a particular frame of mind, an entrepreneur's frame of mind, knowing it doesn't matter what the opportunity is, but you'll pursue it until you realize that it's not a good opportunity. You'll do as much as you can to check it out.

You have to be able to deal with rejection and failure. You have to be able to take responsibility for your decisions. When you're a businessman, you make decisions: sometimes they're bad ones, and that's too bad, but you have to know how to make them. You have to be good at that. You have to be honest too. And love people. If you don't love people you won't sell much jewelry.

The reason it's very hard for many people to sell is that they can't stand to hear the word *no*. It's very easy for me to hear it. It doesn't bother me at all. When I sell jewelry, I don't care if somebody doesn't want to buy from me, because somebody else will. So I'm just nice to people. I give out free candy and Coca-Cola to everybody, whether they buy jewelry from me or not.

When people say, "I don't want to buy anything from you. See you later," I say, "See you later." I'm happy, and they're happy because they exercised their freedom of choice. I don't try to make them feel guilty. Doing that is self-defeating, because it doesn't make them feel any better and it doesn't make you feel any better. And you still don't make the sale.

If you want to be in business you have to be prepared to face rejection. At the same time you have to realize that there are certain laws, which every good salesman and every good businessman knows are true, that will work for them in the end. One of those laws is that it all comes down to numbers.

With any retail business, location is very key. In Saint Thomas, when I was selling jewelry, hundreds and hundreds of people each day came to where I was selling jewelry. So the numbers worked for me. I was outside, at an eighteen-foot-long stand, and I was the only one who could sell anything on this platform with a beautiful view. It was one of the most beautiful places I've ever been. It was great. Despite the high rent, the numbers worked for me, and at the end of the day I would have $1,000.

Once I got back here I also started a dance-class business. I didn't know how to jitterbug, but I met a girl who did; I got her to be my partner and we put together a school and hired teachers and everything. We did it for two years. Business was pretty good; it was a lot of fun, and I learned how to jitterbug.

It wasn't hard to set up the dance business. I had to register with the city of Cambridge, rent a place to hold the classes, and take out ads, but I hired somebody to do all that. I auditioned the teachers myself. I didn't have to incorporate. "Tahiti Ted" was incorporated, but I'm not anymore because there isn't any good reason, taxwise, to be incorporated, and there wasn't any other reason at all.

Another thing I would recommend to people who want to go into business is first to learn elementary bookkeeping because it's absolutely essential to know whether you're making money. How much you take in is important. Down in Saint Thomas, I took in a lot of money, but I wasn't actually making as much as I thought I was because I hadn't learned bookkeeping; I learned the next summer. I did not know how to do a basic income statement, where you take your sales, subtract your cost of goods sold — which is your gross profit — then subtract all your expenses — which gives you your net profit. That's the only number that's of any real consequence in business. The bottom line. You've got to know what that is. Because you take in all this money, you see it in your hand, you say, "WOW, look at all this money!" But, in reality, at the end of the month you've had your overhead for your rent and all the other things that people never think about when they decide to go into business. These are not reasons not to go into business; they are reasons to learn bookkeeping.

The main thing is that you can learn from your mistakes. Anytime I've made a mistake I've had the attitude that it's just "growth and development." I might have a bad growth and development day, or a bad growth and development year, perhaps, but those are mistakes I hope I won't make again.

Once more, I strongly recommend to people that they love their customers and treat them with love.

As for the future, I may come back here some day and go to the Business School, where my grandfather was once the dean. But to be successful in business is only one of my three goals in life. The other two are to get married and have lots of kids, and to prevent a nuclear war, if I can. For the last few months I've been writing a book, proposing a constitutional amendment to ban nuclear war. This is more important to me than being a success in business. But you do have to eat. As long as I can behave normally, I believe in being a businessman.

GAME PLAN To Retail South Sea Island Jewelry

A. Market: Impulse buying by individuals.

  1. Approach: To set up sidewalk vendor stands where there was a heavy flow of traffic.

B. Competition: Other vendors.

C. Goods and Overhead

  1. Materials: Delicate island jewelry.
  2. Equipment: Sidewalk vendor tables.
  3. Facilities: Rental for location in Saint Thomas, $3,500 per month.

D. Capital: Capital is needed to purchase the jewelry and to cover overhead — equipment, facilities, and licenses.

1. Cash flow: A possible $1,000 in gross sales per day. Total costs for materials and overhead should be considered when determining cash flow versus profit.

E. Regulations: Licenses may have to be obtained for vending and/or operating a retail business (depending on local laws and customs).

F. Risk
   1. Financial: The liquidity of jewelry, especially unique jewelry, minimizes financial risks.

G. Time Commitment: Once the contacts for obtaining the jewelry have been arranged, the tasks of selling and bookkeeping are flexible.

H. What's Involved
   1. Securing a supply and the means of distribution.
   2. Selecting a choice location.
   3. Complying with regulations.
   4. Marketing the goods.
   5. "Loving everybody."

Ted doesn't go into it at any length, but a little bit of showmanship doesn't exactly hurt a sidewalk vendor. When you approach one of Tahiti Ted's stands to look at his jewelry, he goes to work on you, giving you his spiel, at the same time filling your pockets with penny candy. You may not buy any jewelry, but you will definitely leave there a sweeter person.

It's important to check out all local regulations very carefully before investing in such items as stock, tables, portable display cases that can be locked, and some form of transportation. In some cities — Washington, D.C., is one of them — the indoor merchants are complaining that the sidewalk sellers — who pay neither rent nor taxes in most cases — have an unfair advantage and keep customers from shopping indoors. The laws in Washington haven't been changed yet, but it would be wise to check them out anywhere before starting a sidewalk stand in an established business area. (When Tahiti Ted sells near the Mall in Washington, where there are no stores, he doesn't have that problem to worry about.)

Always remember the first rule of sidewalk selling: location is key. The next rule, at least according to Ted, is love your customers. That doesn't hurt either.

Portrait of the Consultant as a Young Man

When I was at college here, six or seven years ago, students were very much into rebelling. But that has changed in the last five years, because of economic woes. I think that young people, whether they go to a public school or a private school, have decided that the load on their parents is just too much for them to bear. So the students are willing to work.

— John Kopchik

At twenty-three, John Kopchik is another "oldie but goodie." About to enter his last year at the Law School, John graduated with the highest honors from the college where he was an Economics major. From a small Indiana town near Gary (where he worked in the steel mills), John has had a variety of jobs. The older he got, the more entrepreneurial the jobs became. His latest venture, a consulting group effort, is unusual in that his partners include several professors.

John preaches a new pragmatism for a new time and speaks eloquently of the benefits — to both sides — of faculty-student ventures. Although some of his work sounds as if it is on a very rarefied level — his latest project involves Japan and robots! — he swears that the idea of students working with professors for profit is one that can be applied anywhere. Still, the reader will notice that John Kopchik is a pretty unusual and accomplished guy.

Five of us got together with a bunch of academics — a couple from the Harvard Business School faculty, a graduate of the Business School, my college roommate, who now works for a consulting group in Boston, and another gentleman. We started a consulting enterprise on robotics, an industry analysis of robots in the industrial workplace. What we essentially did was to make two major analyses, one of Japanese robots in the United States and one of American producers'.

We're finding a bunch of problems from legal and labor-relations standpoints, as well as from an economic cost analysis. We think that this type of consulting is going to be the wave of the future. We've made some money doing the report, and we're very happy with it. I think it gave us good experience. What we've done is sort of a small version of management consulting. We do sectoral analyses along the lines of the Harvard Business School. We have some nice connections with the Business School and the Boston consulting community.

If there's one thing we're certain of, it's that robots will play an increasingly larger part in industry. There are 40,000 in the world today, and experts expect that number to triple by 1990. Worker displacement, especially in places like Detroit, has become a big social issue. Most robots today are in the automotive and aerospace industries, basically doing assembly.

But the thing to remember is that a robot is a link between the microprocessor mind of the computer and the machine tool. It's like giving flesh, mobility, and movement to a computer.

There's a lot to be learned about the legal and labor-relations implications behind the application of robots from a comparison basis: robots don't strike; they never get tired; they win back their investment in one and one-third years; they never talk to other workers; they don't have to be retired or paid a pension; they don't drink; and so on. I've been involved in a lot of work at the Harvard Law School with a professor who is an expert on Japan.

I've been doing this type of consulting for up to thirty hours a week, and it's paying my way through school.

One thing I'd like to stress, especially for students who don't have a lot of capital, is that many of the people I work with are too busy and too "big name" to sit around drafting reports. However, they don't mind kicking in a couple of hundred thousand dollars to a Subchapter S corporation. This allows them, legally, to write off the losses on, say, gathering information for the first year or, as in our case, November and December of the closing tax year. This money is spent for the promise of gain in the years to follow and a share in the company. Those who donated the bulk of the money got a large interest in the company; they gave us cash up front for equipment, such as a word processor, and paid our expenses to go to Connecticut and Ohio to do interviews as part of a field study, for long-distance phone calls, and for the incredible costs of starting up.

Duplicating what we have done should not be all that hard, especially in a big university context like this, where people are always moving in and out. Having academic credence you can translate into the business world helps a lot. There's no substitute for energy, or for getting together with people you know and trust and trying to get something like this off the ground.

Don't be shy. I think that marketing is 99 percent of the game. The idea is out there, a brooding omnipresence that you can pick out, but I think that the guts and the sweat and the nerve are really something that only you can supply. Any university community has a lot of labor available, people trained in specific tasks, which can be put to use by those who are later along in life and more established and who can spare funds for start-up costs for a tax write-off that later translates into a share of the company.

There are many industries in which you don't need a hundred thousand dollars. You may need only a couple of thousand that investors will provide as long as you have academic credence within your community. If a professor who's writing on the industrial takeover by robots knows someone who took his course, is really interested in the subject and got an *A*, I don't see any problem at all in his gathering a couple of people who are interested in different facets of it to work for him. Nor do I see anything wrong with students asking the professor for the names of others he may know who are interested in doing a report on that topic.

Now, not everyone agrees with me on that idea. There are those who say that college is meant to be enjoyed and one should have time to be young, or that the idea raises conflicts that might be unethical. But it seems to me that as long as a kid who is struggling to get through school, as I was, is paid for his endeavors and retains his interest in a fascinating subject, it's all for the better. It's interesting that as funding tightens up and financial aid shrinks, more and more resources within the school that are not considered financial aid open up for students to earn a living. In the Law School, the most striking example is the number of professors who hire students for summer research jobs.

It's a pragmatism that could come into some criticism for conflict of interest, but it also shows that people really care about students getting through a place like this, where the costs are enormous.

I've had a lot of experience with the Entrepreneurs club, and it's very interesting to me that the great majority of members come up with ideas that are somehow related to inspirations they get from a professor or a course or an academic environment. Even if the idea doesn't come directly from the academic environment, the associations made in that environment, I would tend to speculate, further the idea. If you hear about an idea for fuel-saving devices, and in your math class there are eight people in the back of the room who can work out the details, that's another way of furthering entrepreneurism. I think in the great majority of cases arrangements can be worked out without a conflict problem.

If my professors hadn't helped, maybe they'd have had

more time to write books or to travel and lecture. But in this instance, they saw that I particularly needed the job to get by, to survive. They got me interested in a topic whose social ramifications just might be the most important industrial topic since the microprocessor and the computer chip. Today we face overarching automation and the loss of jobs: Where are you going to put people? When you link up computers and make them mobile, with functional capabilities that allow them to move around and do jobs, and put sensors on them so they can feel and touch and hear, then you really have to analyze the issues. In the broader sense, they opened me up to something that I would have never seen. In a place like this, you get your degree, hear the standard logic, the economics of it, and you pass through without ever having to think. When I went to the robotics convention in Detroit, I saw the unemployment there. Outside the beautiful hotel where the convention was held people with nothing to do were milling around, some of them even begging. That really brought it home to me.

The whole project has really opened my eyes, and I hope the work we do shows that there are two sides to the question. I went into it thinking that professors would pay me to write an efficiency argument, and I'm coming out learning so much more about the equity. It helped me to see a broader view of the world.

Many of the professors who get involved in situations like this trade their services to corporations, say, in exchange for the corporations' help in finding jobs and work opportunities for students. That strikes me as a lot more altruistic and interesting. And helpful.

There is a lot of this activity at other places — Stanford, for example. But at Harvard, I think the law professors have been very good about placing people, getting them term-time work, interviewing for clerkships, making sure they get the right idea about prospective jobs. People are very job-oriented.

The attitude toward jobs has changed drastically since I was a Harvard freshman. People realize that it's not a loss of your innocence or a loss of your free time to do something that is not exactly graded. I think you can learn a lot from that too.

I earned my way through the college doing work at the National Bureau of Economic Research and as a research assistant at the Business School. So I've been doing quantitative ec stuff for about six years now.

One of the most wonderful things in my business experience is that I've met people who helped me to learn that college wasn't the stiff, formal experience I'd expected it to be. I graduated Phi Beta Kappa, but working didn't hurt me in the least. I think it helped me to get a better idea of the world.

How much a student should work outside of class is of course a matter of degree, but a lot of work experience can be especially helpful. And I think, particularly at Harvard, where a lot of the students have never had to work, it might even be important to make it mandatory!

There are many more kids doing business things today. When I was here back in the mid-1970s, I'd say maybe 5 percent of the people I knew were doing something. Right now, I'd say it's up to 15 percent. It's easily tripled. I think it's a sign of the times, but I don't think you have to be an academic sellout to do something economically profitable.

You *need* that other experience. I think it was Lyndon Johnson who said, "I'd trust him a lot more if he won for county sheriff one time." He was talking about all the pinheads who sat around in cabinet meetings. I meet all these people who are great technical analysts, but I'd feel a lot more comfortable if they had to sell roses on the corner for one day in their lives.

There couldn't have been a Harvard Entrepreneurs club when I was a freshman in 1976. It wouldn't have been "cool," and it would definitely have been "nonmajoritarian" and "nonprogressive." It would have been considered capitalist.

I think that people in college — say, under twenty-one — are satisfied with less of a return, and the only thing they lack is a sort of cynicism.

Everyone I know who's over twenty-one has gone

through one friend's, or his or her own, failure in a business or two. It's like getting your first *C* on a report card — it comes in everyone's life, but after the first one it never feels the same. That's the thing. Young people are not suspicious, or *as* suspicious, and they're not as cynical.

I work as an advisor for freshmen here, which can be tough, but the one thing I enjoy is hearing students out about their personal qualms regarding business and academics. "Am I taking too much away from my studies? Am I taking a lighter course load because of this?"

These are real concerns and questions that deserve to be listened to. I try to inject a little realism, economically speaking, while trying to give them some intellectual idealism.

I think it's been wonderful. I'm really happy.

GAME PLAN To Work with or for Professors

A. Market: Academicians who need or welcome assistance.

    1. Approach: Ask a professor for a job.
    2. Price: Varies considerably.

B. Competition: There are plenty of opportunities available to those who have the ability to market their own talents.

C. Goods and Overhead: These will usually be provided for you.

D. Capital: The student needs no money of his own to get involved in such an enterprise. However, if and when the venture needs to be funded, there are tax breaks (see IRS information on Subchapter S corporations).

E. Regulation: The concept of professors and their students engaging in commercial pursuits together is still a debatable idea. However, most institutions

publish guidelines that should answer most
questions of an ethical nature.

F. Time Commitment: Most arrangements average
about fifteen hours a week, but this time can, and
often does, double.

G. What's Involved

1. Identifying professors whose expertise
complements your own interests.
2. Marketing your skills to the professor.
3. "Sweat and nerve" in fulfilling your
commitment to the venture.

As John Kopchik says, "It's a pragmatism that could
come into some criticism for conflict of interest." True,
but it is also a concept that can provide great good for
any number of people — students, professors, and the
public that is served by the results of their joint ventures.

What is so exciting about John's idea, and experience,
is that it can be copied by any student or group of students at any college or university in the nation. And think
of all the areas in which it can be used! The new devel-
opments in human engineering may be a bit too esoteric,
but there are countless other areas in which the combination of the professors' expertise and contacts and the
students' intelligence and hard work can provide exciting
results.

Remember Kopchik's motto: Don't be shy!

BOOK THREE

"WOW!" or You Too Can Be an Undergraduate Mogul

1
$E^2 = E^2$ = Welcome to Fuel Tech

Unlike Mr. Wilson at Data Acquisition, Mr. Haney, a founding member of the Harvard Entrepreneurs Society, thrives on the marketing end of the product. A History of Science major, he first stumbled on the device, not in the laboratory, but through Mr. Gazvoda, Entrepreneurs' president, who is now sales director of Fuel Tech. Mr. Gazvoda saw a sign on the Boston subway touting the invention.

Both he and Mr. Haney approached the inventor, checked his credentials, ran a few tests on the platinum-based device, and bought him out. The two students rounded up some venture capital, opened a Cambridge office, and hired a sales force of four.

Now Fuel Tech boasts five employees, a modest full-time Washington office, a Canadian subsidiary, Atlantic Fuel Tech, and some solid customers.

The company has drawn the attention of several professors on campus, and is looked on as a sound bet to go in the black next year. Professor Chandler of the Business School gives Fuel Tech high marks. "There is definitely something there, something lasting," he said.

New York Times
January 17, 1982

How simple and almost easy it sounds when the history of Fuel Tech is so neatly and briefly summarized. That, of course, is the way it must look to any outsider, anyone who wasn't there through all the fits and starts and almost stops that lie behind the office doors of any new company. The expanded version of the Fuel Tech story is a lot more complicated and a lot less certain of success, but the fact remains that we have — like the other undergraduate business ventures described in the *Times* story — turned an idea into a real business. We are including the Fuel Tech story in this section so that you, the reader, can see what we did in case you are interested in doing something similar. Your idea may have nothing to do with energy, and you may favor a larger or smaller type of operation, but we feel that by learning about what we went through you will be better able to gauge your own chances of success. As you read, keep one thing in mind: we had never tried anything on this scale before, yet we made it go. So can you.

One February afternoon in 1981, riding a subway train between Cambridge and Boston on the way to price roses, Ed saw an advertisement for a fuel-saving device that intrigued him. He jotted down the number. (This was about the same time we were setting up the Entrepreneurs club, and we'd heard a lot about fuel- and energy-saving companies as "hot" ideas for new businesses.)

The phone number led us to a meeting with Mr. Joel Robinson, a man who had invented not one, but two, fuel-saving devices, one rather small and the other quite a bit larger. The first device, called the "GasSaver," which sold for about $20 retail and half of that wholesale, was used to increase the fuel efficiency of automobiles. The second, called the "FuelSaver," was connected to large steam boilers to make the water boil sooner, thereby saving the fuel used to heat it to the boiling point. Initially, because we were so interested in the GasSaver, we paid little attention to the other device.

Mr. Robinson had said that the GasSaver would produce a "guaranteed 20 percent saving." We took a sample to a Nobel Prize–winning professor who said it "looked worth testing." Ed borrowed some money from his father and we bought eighty-seven units. We installed several of them and began to receive test results. We were pleased. In fact, we began — and probably everyone does this at the beginning of any business — to calculate how much we would make if the device tested out. We thought that if we worked like crazy we might be able to sell four hundred units, which would bring us $16,000. With that money we could live on the Cape all summer. That was our first dream.

Then the first solid test results came in, and we were stunned: the devices produced average fuel-consumption savings of 28 percent. Our dream escalated until we got to the point of seeing ourselves outside the door of King Tut's tomb.

We were stunned a second time when we checked out, through automotive jobbers who service the large chain automotive stores, the potential sales based on the number of units that could be made each month. If we found an established company to market the product and charged only a 10 percent finder's fee, we stood to make millions of dollars. And if we marketed it ourselves the figures rose to the *hundreds of millions*!

Reality set in, however, when we learned that the inventor's price for the exclusive rights to market the GasSaver was $500,000! Although we actually tried to raise the money — we had met some people around campus who claimed to know the kind of people who loaned that kind of money — it turned out to be a hopeless task. We could raise some money, but not nearly enough, and the inventor would not lower his price.

At about this point we began to think maybe we'd been after the wrong invention. As attracted as we were to the GasSaver, it would have meant dealing with huge numbers of individual purchasers. But the FuelSaver, though its selling price would have to be far greater, would have the advantage of requiring us to deal with scientific and technical people. As both our fathers said, the automotive sales field was very fast-paced, but breaking into the field of selling boiler units to companies and schools was actually more plausible. Instead of a long-shot chance at making $100 million, we might have a more realistic chance of making $1 million.

We began to talk to the inventor about marketing the FuelSaver. This time we knew that when we went out to try to raise money from the sophisticated financial types, we had better get our act together and put something down on paper. Within days we were immersed in such previously unknown items as patent opinions.

The tests on the FuelSaver (a name we didn't like and planned to change as soon as possible if we got the rights to it) were also very impressive, showing savings in fuel consumption ranging from 12 percent to 41 percent. Once people began to hear that, we started to hear from potential investors, and we made a deal with one of them. He put up enough money for start-up costs, and we rented a three-room office suite that is convenient to school and our rooms.

As our first two official acts, we changed the name of the device from the FuelSaver to the "Platinum Delivery System," and we called the company something far simpler and easier to remember — Fuel Tech. We were in business.

(We must point out that none of us had any special training, skill, or relevant experience at this time. We knew nothing about boilers, platinum, combustion, and very little about sales. We knew only that we believed in the product and in our ability to sell it. We had no idea of the amount and intensity of the work that lay ahead of us.)

By the fall we had spent a good part of the original investment capital, but had also made some sales. One was to Portsmouth Abbey, Bill's alma mater, which had reported substantial savings that heartened us. We also made a sale to Boston College, but that one did not work out as well because we weren't able to test it properly.

When the original seed capital of $10,000 was about to run out, we were approached by Walter Burr, a student and friend who had been helping out in the office and had come to like what he saw. He knew someone who was interested in investing, and in December we signed an agreement that provided an immediate loan to Fuel Tech of $60,000. It also provided that twice that much, $120,000, be set aside to be loaned to us in the future, by a certain date, *but only if we had met certain conditions by then*. (This is, as most readers probably know, called an escrow agreement.) The conditions were that we had to get a strong opinion from a reputable patent-law firm (saying the invention was the legal property of the inventor and no one else), and that we had to buy the patent from Mr. Robinson. The time period during which we were to meet the terms of the escrow agreement was four months.

We charged ahead with renewed enthusiasm, and our sales picture soon reflected it. Columbia and Harvard were trying the device; Boston College and Portsmouth Abbey had already bought it; and tests were under way at Abrams Management, Howard and American universities in Washington, D.C., and Corning Glass in Corning, New York. We also had some sales activity in Canada.

Not everything was coming up roses, however (or, considering Ed's experience with that particular flower, maybe things were running true to form). Wrapping up the contract negotiations with the inventor turned out to be an arduous task. Both "sides" had to hire lawyers, and the document that resulted ran to at least sixteen pages. Every point had to be resolved to the satisfaction of three parties — Fuel Tech, Mr. Robinson, and the lawyers. (Make that four parties.) Plus, everything had to fit the stringent terms of the escrow agreement. Something we thought could be hashed out in a week or two took us almost to the end of the four-month escrow period. And the whole process cost us $15,000 in legal fees!

Mr. Robinson did sign, but, unfortunately, that did not end our problems because we didn't meet all the terms of the escrow agreement; therefore we didn't have the money necessary to follow through on the terms of the contract. In other words, we couldn't pay him. He was beginning to talk about dropping the whole thing, which he had the right to do if he didn't get paid. What's more, we'd been so busy with the contract negotiations that we'd neglected our customers, and some of them were not too happy.

And if that wasn't enough, all of this took place during our midterm exam period, that delightful time of year when Harvard makes you prove you are part of the student body, and Bill was in the hospital for two weeks, getting his "hockey shoulders" repaired. It was *not* a fun time.

One of our big problems at the time — and anybody who gets involved in a well-financed business (whether the money comes from personal funds, investors, or a bank loan) should be aware of this problem — was that we had an awful lot of friendly advisers whose advice turned out to be questionable, at best. We were under the impression that just around the corner were any number of wealthy investors ready to pump a million dollars' worth of life into Fuel Tech.

Having been there, we would also warn other people our age starting out in business that there is a tendency to rely on the advice of older people simply because they are older and supposedly more experienced. We hired too many consultants twice our age and learned, the hard way, to check things out for ourselves. We would have been a lot better off just keeping the whole thing simple.

Then, in a burst of pure serendipity, when things looked dark, everything changed for the better. Several people went on vacation, some cut back their involvement to concentrate on school, and suddenly the company was speaking with one voice. The escrow agreement problems were worked out, and the money "dropped," which solved any number of related problems. So, we had the contract, money in the bank, and a better organization internally. As a result, sales began to improve. Finally, the company was beginning to look like a real company.

One of our biggest problems at the start, and it's something you should be very careful to avoid, is that we had all chiefs and no Indians. There was no real leader, and because everyone who was in on Fuel Tech at the beginning had substantial portions of stock, it would have been hard to fire anybody. Too many business decisions that should have been simple to make became the basis for *extended* discussion among four or five strong personalities. We even ran into the problem of having decisions become "unmade" because someone had a new thought. We called that the "waffle syndrome."

We solved one problem coming out of this bad period by making just one of us (Bill) the person in sole charge of Fuel Tech, the chief executive officer, in effect. That turned out to be the smartest decision we made because it meant that day-to-day matters, plus almost all of the others, could be handled without having to call a board meeting to reach a "consensus." As a result of that decision, and the fact that several other people decided to put their main efforts elsewhere, the company emerged looking leaner and more efficient — and that appealed to the moneylenders who were waiting in the wings.

Not too long after we got everything straightened out and humming, the article appeared in the *New York Times,* increasing the number of inquiries and calls from people needing help — inventors, money people looking to invest, or people with ventures like Fuel Tech who wanted us to manage them. What's more, we had students calling every week, wanting to work with or for us, and *corporations* calling to see if we would develop products for them or send students from the club to help with their management. There were a lot of calls from people who wanted us to put the finishing touches on their ideas and make them work. As might be expected, we chased down some pretty harebrained ideas; but they all showed the great interest that exists in entrepreneurism.

So Fuel Tech moved out of its infancy and began to walk on its own. Each important new step was steadier than the one before it. We renegotiated our contract with Mr. Robinson; we rearranged the stock ownership to be more consistent with the time commitment; and we were able to hire new management: a Ph.D. in chemical engineering who'd designed boilers; a marketing specialist who'd spent years with a leading combustion company; and a five-person service group that has had years of experience in specialized trouble-shooting. Finally, we worked on improving the product (for the fourth time!) and have paid close attention to "customer feedback."

Over the next twelve months, if we meet all our projected sales figures, we will pay out, in salaries, something like $400,000! But then, if that happens, our sales will be in the millions of dollars.

We believe we can meet these goals because we now have extensive testing programs with such giants as Corning Glass and General Motors, plus strong possibilities with Bacardi, United Shoe Manufacturers, and Columbia University. The possible earnings, should all of these possibilities work out, could be from $6 to $10 million.

(It may be informative to explain that our charges are based on the number of burners, and their size, in a given facility. For example, if General Motors buys our unit for one of their boilers it would be worth $36,000 a month to us; if they buy it for eight boilers, that would mean *$250,000* a month. What's more, as part of our price arrangement we get a small percentage of the company's annual fuel bill. Considering that some of the companies we have been dealing with have yearly fuel bills in the tens of millions of dollars, it is clear that we are in a growth industry. Indeed, annual fuel bills in our industry are in the $15 *billion* range.)

The biggest compliment to Fuel Tech is that the new people we brought in, those with industry experience, all took pay cuts. *But,* they have shares in this company, which they didn't have before, and an escalating pay scale. So they have a goal that will make all the extra work worthwhile.

The "bottom line" is that Fuel Tech has grown into something far greater than just the dream of a couple of entrepreneurial college kids.

GAME PLAN To Market a Patented System That (Cost-Effectively) Increases Boiler Efficiency

A. Market: Industrial consumers of fossil fuels.

1. Approach: To target sales efforts to large consumers of fuel, i.e., power plants, ships, factories.
2. Price: The price varies, depending on the quantity of combustibles treated; yet the cost is normally half the savings and requires no capital expenditure on the part of the consumer.
3. Timing: The service provides an immediate windfall for the consumer, so any time of the year, especially before the heating season, is the time to approach targeted accounts.

B. Competition: Numerous fuel-additive products do exist; yet according to our studies, they cannot

match the cost-effectiveness or achieve 5 percent
to 10 percent fuel savings on industrial boilers.
Fuel Tech uses a precious-metal catalyst, which we
consider to be superior to the additives used by
other energy-saving companies.

C. Goods and Overhead
   1. Materials: Precious-metal catalyst.
   2. Equipment: Analytical devices for boilers.
   3. Facilities: An office to serve as headquarters
      for the entire operation.

D. Capital: Fuel Tech has already raised close to a
   million dollars to finance its operation. Currently, it
   is privately soliciting an additional $450,000.

E. Regulations: Fuel Tech must comply with a host of
   Securities and Exchange Commission (S.E.C.),
   state, local, and federal regulations.

F. Risk
   1. Financial: The risk is viewed as minimal at the
      current stage of development; but, at times, the
      possibility of the company's "liquidation" has
      been real.

G. Time Commitment: The company has required a
   great deal of time and hustle to get where it is
   today. As the company continues to grow and
   succeed, the time involvement rises geometrically.

H. What's Involved
   1. Locating a marketable product.
   2. Securing rights to the product.
   3. Legally protecting the product and company.
   4. Raising capital.
   5. Marketing the product.
   6. Performing a myriad of tasks: hiring,
      bookkeeping, research and development, and
      many, many more.

In forming an energy-saving company, we wasted an enormous amount of personal energy. Our advice to anyone interested in setting up a large business venture would be to take a more realistic view of your plans and the potential difficulties involved than we did. However, that said, we should also mention that you will probably make many of the same kinds of mistakes we made, simply because optimism is common to entrepreneurs, and "hope springs eternal." That doesn't mean you have to make those mistakes, though. At the end of the book we present a sample market plan, which is exactly the kind of instrument we needed to know how to draw up at the beginning — and did not. If you want to take one good lesson from our experience, it would be to learn how to make a market plan before you are in the midst of what should be carefully planned activity.

Another point worth thinking about early on is how many of your friends and buddies should be part of your company. In most cases, as businesses shake down, it turns out that looking for a stranger with the right experience would probably have been a wiser move (but one that is hard to do at the time). Fortunately, we didn't lose any friends in the process of creating Fuel Tech, but it could have happened, and that would have been most unfortunate.

Finally, beware of people who offer financing but in return want to take such a large part of your stock or ownership that your company is not really yours anymore. We ran into — and away from — a lot of people like that. If it's yours, keep it yours.

2

A Few Biggies

The people you are about to meet are impressive. They represent the superstar level of our campus's economic and entrepreneurial life. In fact, their accomplishments moved us to put them in a category all by themselves. But we did that to honor them, and by no means to intimidate you. For the underlying theme of this book remains the same — that *you* can do it, that you don't need any special skills, or status, or privilege to be successful in your own business. Hard work and perseverance count most of all.

At the moment, Fuel Tech looks like a pretty good bet; by the time you read this we may be *very* pleased with it. But the only real reason it is so relatively healthy today is that we stuck with it, and stuck with ourselves, and with our belief in ourselves. We had to learn as we went; we did not go into the business with a backlog of knowledge and experience. There is no reason you can't do the same thing if you want to.

The five people you will meet in this chapter represent an interesting cross section of university life. Three are seniors and two juniors. Of the five, only one went to a prep school. The rest are public high school graduates. Two of them are Economics majors, two Biology, and one government. Three are from the East Coast (New York City, New York State, and Massachusetts), one is from the Midwest (Minnesota), and one is from the Virgin Islands. Three are white, one is black, and the other is from India.

Although their accomplishments are as diverse as they are, all share two things — a belief in themselves and a great deal of optimism.

From Poker Player to Broker: *Jim Azzarito*

Jim Azzarito, a twenty-one-year-old junior, is from Newburyport, Massachusetts, a small seacoast town near the New Hampshire line, a town that he says is now becoming "chic." An Economics major who specializes in "industrial organization/managerial economics," Jim does not specialize in his entrepreneurial activities: he has not one but three separate ventures, each of which has a solid potential.

A self-proclaimed risk-taker, Jim claims to be a very good poker player, and has been known to spend "entire summers at the race track." He kids Ed about which one of them has had more jobs. Unlike Tahiti Ted, Azzarito does not insist on loving people, but he does believe that the key to success in business is understanding them.

I've always more or less liked investments, real estate mostly. And the reason for that, basically, is that it's about the easiest to go into. It's pretty nuts-and-boltsy.

Around June or July of 1981 I was pretty hot to do something in real estate. I had been in investments before, but never in real estate. Also, I had spent a lot of time the last three years in state government jobs and I was pretty familiar with the Human Services network. My partners and I had gotten wind of a deal on a nursing home in Haverhill, which looked pretty good. That turned out to be the first deal we ever got into.

In July of that year, based on my knowledge of the procedures involved, which I'd gained by working for the state, I set up a real estate holding corporation, to hold the actual commercial property. I also set up Church View Health Center, which actually operates the nursing home and in which I am a one-third partner. I was aware of this need because of my background with the state, which is something anybody else can get.

I'd originally gotten into a state consulting job through student government. There's a state student government organization in Massachusetts that is organized around high school students; it's a really big organization, and I had been the chairman of it. Also I had met various state people by doing "Outreach."

I think that's the best way for students to go to get experience, because the private sector is a little harder to get into, in the sense of being allowed to do anything responsible. The nursing home deal rests heavily on my having made all those contacts and done all that work so that I was familiar with the rules and regulations. The big hassle was with the licensing.

I went into the nursing home deal with two partners. One of them was very good with grants; the other one had a nursing home license; and they were both entrepreneurs in other areas.

The concept of entrepreneur, at least for me, is a broker who matches the right bodies with the right pools of money, lets it happen until it's going at its own speed, and then lets go.

The important thing in nursing homes is to understand Medicare funding and the kinds of mechanisms that underlie rate setting. An awful lot of licensing activities go on. Massachusetts is definitely the leader in that area. And some of the stuff is pretty wild. The fire marshal will come in and tell you to do this, and then the state EPA guy will come in and say do that, so we spend a lot of our time trying to satisfy them, trying to keep all the different bodies happy. Having seen these agencies from the inside, I find it pretty interesting now to see them from the other side.

Entrepreneurism is either exciting to you or scary, because you do put yourself out on the line. I had no money at all. What little I had and what I was able to convince my parents to put up was right out there the first few months. It could have folded up pretty easily.

But now, looking back, I realize that I am a very wise investor!

Poker — and I think I'm a really good poker player — is probably a good analogy for all this business stuff. There's a lot of psychology involved, especially in buying and selling, picking your managers, doing the personnel stuff, and trying to find a lawyer who's worth working with. As an economist, I've learned all the investment theory here at Harvard, the microeconomics and the macroeconomics, what's happening in the government, and the capital situation. But I think the really important thing is understanding people. What makes them excited, what makes them tick, and how to get them interested in what you're doing and how to get them to go along.

A lot of people out there, however, take a different tack; they need someone else to show them the way to go. They would be scared to death to try to start anything up themselves. When I'm fifty, or whatever, with four kids, I'm not going to be as interested in going out and trying these projects.

It's pretty easy to sell out here. When I came in I was going to be pre-med. If you get your C's, and then go to Fred's Medical School, you can go back to your hometown and make your $60,000 to $70,000 a year, and everyone thinks you're wonderful. A lot of people are into that, and I came pretty close to doing it. But then, if money is your motivation, you come to the conclusion that there are other things you can do to make a lot more of it and also enjoy yourself.

This stuff I'm doing is a lot of fun. When the weather warms up I start getting excited.

We have a really hot condominium project that looks possible for us to put together. It's in the same geographical area, and being able to realize its potential is really the benefit of having some of our experience. It's an eight-unit building that we're probably going to be able to pick up for about $15,000. Now, we'll have to put another $150,000 or $200,000 into it, but we'll be able to borrow that money. We may be able to get federal bucks to do it, at low interest, long term. And if we do, WOW!

It's a lot like going to the race track. You put your money down — and it ought to be money that you can lose without starving — and then it's gone and you take it from there.

What excites me is that the nursing home and the real estate setup are now valued at at least $150,000, but I only risked about $2,000 of my own money.

The third phase of my operation is an adolescent care center that we're starting, which is going to be funded by the Department of Mental Health, among other agencies. It's got a capacity of eight adolescents right now, and is located in a leased property in Haverhill. We may have to buy a property; in fact, that may be the way I swing the condominium thing.

This is another instance in which the state experience can really begin to pay off. I know people in all the agencies that will be involved. In fact, we recently sat down with our lawyer and got a renewal of an $80,000 grant that an agency was trying to keep from us. I don't think we could have done that without our experience. They were trying to outstare us and we ended up outstaring them. It was neat.

If you understand the ropes, you could probably get away with running a lousy program and even making a lot of money at it, but I don't think you could do that long term. Certainly not after meeting the people for whom you're setting up the project. If you did, you couldn't sleep at night.

I do the major real estate deals, the big personnel stuff, and some of the financial dealings. I look at the tax picture. But expert consultants handle the rest. The important thing is to bring in people who know what is going on. As for the people who are running things for you, you either have faith in them or you don't. You set up the format, bring the people together, and then let it go. You have to have enough discipline to pull away.

I know a lot about the business now, but in the beginning it was kind of a brokerage function. I originally looked at the whole thing as a real estate proposition, so I guess my accurate label would be real estate entrepreneur.

GAME PLAN To Leverage Capital to Obtain Real Estate

A. Market: Private and public property in the Newburyport, Massachusetts, area.

   1. Approach: An insider's advantage to the market demand, since the market area has been his residence.

   2. Price: Varies according to individual property.

   3. Timing: Requires acting quickly to close on desired property.

B. Competition: Other real estate buyers after the same market.

C. Capital: Securing financing to purchase the real estate is the key to success.

D. Regulations: Once a property has been acquired, a host of regulatory agencies must be satisfied with the operation of services and the building's condition.

E. Risk

   1. Financial: The risk is minimal, because of the nature of the real estate market. However, judgment errors with regard to demand for a particular service or regulatory measures that affect the demand for the property may result in a financial loss.

F. What's Involved

   1. Speculating on the real estate market.

   2. Selecting real estate for purchase.

   3. Securing financing for the purchase of the property.

   4. Preparing the property to generate income.

Jim Azzarito mentioned what must sound like a dream to many entrepreneur types — that he had parlayed a $2,000 personal investment into two businesses worth

$150,000 to $200,000. However, don't miss the point that Azzarito had prepared himself to take advantage of the opportunity through his knowledge of state regulations gained by working for the state. He had met many important people on the state level because he had spent a lot of time in student government. Not too many "fortunes" are made by luck and nothing else. Notice too that his partners have experience in areas other than his own, and that he chose them for just that reason. He talks about luck and loving to gamble, but his approach is actually very businesslike. Remember, he says, that whatever money you risk "ought to be money that you can lose without starving." Jim Azzarito also gives very good advice to certain types of entrepreneurs — those who love the creation but can't stand the day-to-day details that follow — when he says that in some cases, once you have a business up and running, you simply have to let go. Azzarito's business advice and philosophy are worth heeding.

Taking Stock: *Jim Carona*

Jim came to Harvard because of basketball, but a funny thing happened on his way to the court. He knew he could score points, but now he realized he could score in a quite different way. Though he's not playing basketball anymore, he keeps himself in great shape (he has a black belt in karate). He makes money for himself and his clients as a stock market analyst and adviser.

Jim Carona is a twenty-one-year-old junior from Albany, New York, a Biology major who may yet end up in med school. But the problem is that his horizons keep expanding. On the day he was interviewed for this book he was all excited because he'd just learned he had won a scholarship to study in France for a year. The market will have to wait. As for Jim's clients, they will undoubt-edly also wait. "My best account this month," he says, "made 78 percent. Overall for the month the average was 42 percent."

I was always interested in the market, even when I was a kid. I started investing when I was in seventh grade.

I went to a public high school in Albany. I came here because I was recruited for basketball. I played as a freshman, but then the time commitment got to be too much. As a freshman, I played sixth man on the varsity, so by now I would have been starting, but when I quit there was no great pressure on me to keep playing. I was surprised.

I don't come from an extremely rich family. I come from a middle-of-the-road family. I personally don't have a lot of money to invest, so this year I got more and more into technical analysis, and I found it was working very, very well.

I became a little frustrated because when I looked at all the information I had been gathering it seemed as if it was going to waste. So I said, "What can I do?" Origi-nally, I was going to write a monthly newsletter, but that idea went down the drain because of the amount of money I would have needed to advertise. I wanted to be a portfolio manager, because that way I wouldn't need any start-up capital. All I need is for people to trust me with their money, which is no easy feat.

I thought about how I would come across to people, and there is one negative aspect — my age. If I tell a man I want to invest $20,000 of his money, he's really going to walk out. I decided that the best technique to use is to give free information. For a limited amount of time, to sort of bait people.

I'm trying to target upper-income, professional people who can afford the risks that I take. I'm very aggressive. I don't hold on to securities very long. I'm a trader, not an investor. As far as I'm concerned, that's the only way you make money in the market.

I gave free information to a few gentlemen that I met — a lawyer and a couple of others. I just mentioned a couple of stocks. Much to my surprise, the lawyer called me within a week and said, "I went on your information, and I put $10,000 on each one you mentioned."

I said, to myself, "Uh-oh." Then I figured out the time period, and I realized that one of the stocks had moved eight points that week and the other had gone up 25 percent. He was very happy about that.

Through his and my father's connections, I built up a small clientele. Now I manage about $100,000. And I've just been elected managing partner of an investment partnership here at Harvard, which manages $60,000.

I'm keeping it as small as I can for now. I don't want to get into the very big numbers because I'm relatively new at working with so much money. I have to get over the mental aspect that I'm moving such large amounts. But I've had a lot of people wanting to get in.

Most people use a technical, fundamental analysis. That means they look at a corporate report, and they decide how that stock is going to do. To me, that's baloney, because it doesn't tell you how the stock's going to do on a day-to-day basis. However, if you use simple techniques dealing with volume and price, you can tell very accurately what a stock is going to do daily.

When I see a stock that is a definite go, I buy it; if it goes up, I sell it on the same day. I make quick profits. It's been working very well, so far.

I had heard that a certain company was about to be taken over, so I told one of my clients to buy in. But for about three weeks nothing happened, and I was kind of "oooh," but when I looked today it had gained 25 percent in the last two days. So I go, "WOW."

My method of operation is based on paying a lot of attention to details. You have to read the *Wall Street Journal* every day because that gives you a good idea of where the market is going. But besides that, all you have to do on any particular stock is chart volume and price. Analysts always chart the price of a stock, but that's where they're wrong. Volume precedes price; the total number of shares is much more important than the price.

Yet only a few people use that method. It's a relatively new theory that's only been around for about seven years. It's a very ingenious technique, and I'm surprised that a lot more people haven't taken it up. But people are very set in their ways. And they resist new ideas.

It is important to realize that what I have done can be done by anyone else who is not afraid to do a lot of research and hard work. That's really all it is. You have to keep your ear to the ground, and you have to associate with people who can help you. I don't think that I could do it all on my own. You have to rely on other people.

So, all this information comes in to me. Now it's my turn to sift everything out. I call the president of every company whose stock I'm studying and get a feel for what he's all about. This is part of my approach, and I don't think many people dig as much as I do. I kind of point my questions at these people. I go to the library. I do a six-month analysis of every stock that I look at, to see where it is technically, where it stands now. I look for little irregularities in each stock, make a chart of it, see what the chart looks like, make trend lines. From all these studies I can make a great assumption about where the stock is heading, where it's going to go.

Back when I started in the market, in the seventh grade, I was just playing. But even then I made some money. There was a stock, Mohawk Data Sciences, that was selling for $1.75 a share. I talked to my father, and he said, "We know some of the people who were involved in that, and it might be a good one." So I got my two hundred dollars out of the bank and bought it. Within a year that stock was over thirty. I was ecstatic over that. Back then I was real excitable — I still am. I remember clearly what I made — two thousand dollars. In six months.

It wasn't until last summer that I really got my feet wet in the market in a serious way. I went into a stock-option deal that fascinated me, even though I know options are very risky and volatile. I got in with a very small investment, and within an hour I had made a thousand dollars. I said to myself, "Do you get out now or do you stay in?" And just like any other stupid, greedy investor, I said, "I'm going to make *twenty* thousand!"

The next day I came in, and watched it on the board; it went down just a slight bit, but I said, "No problem, it'll go back up." Well, within half an hour I dropped that thousand dollars.

Right then I realized where people make their mistake in investing. There are two mistakes. One, you can't make a million on every investment; when you get a nice figure, cut it. Twenty percent. Now, 20 percent is *nice*. You can't get 20 percent anywhere else. The second mistake is that, in general, people buy when the stock is too high. They look at a stock and say, "That one has been *rising*. That one looks good."

You have to look for a stock that people are accumulating slowly. Where you see accumulation, the price is going to rise. If people are getting rid of the stock, slowly, slowly, the stock is going to go down. It's a very subtle technique, very interesting.

The point is that anybody who wants to take the time to learn the process and put in the time to follow the market could do what I'm doing. Initially, I read a few books, strictly technical analyses. The first time I read them — I'm speaking now in particular of Joseph Granville's market-strategy book — I was a little bit fuzzy. But this semester I wrote a thirty-page paper on it, a technical analysis, which I may try to publish, and after that I really understood it. Granville is phenomenal, just phenomenal.

Soon I'm going to advertise and give classes in stock market analysis, and see how that works. That should be fun too.

My parents have been solidly behind me, especially my dad, who is very much go-for-it. My mother is a little more hesitant, but the funny thing is that she is the one who is going to go into business alone, selling women's clothes. It's kind of funny the way it came about, as an extension of my work.

Because of information I gave to some gentlemen, they

told my lawyer about a fashion designer who had name-brand apparel and wanted to sell it to someone. My lawyer suggested my mom. So she's getting into that and it should be very interesting.

I think other people can make money just as I did. You have to have a little intuition, but experience is a big teacher. Also, you have to have some good people around you; you can't rely on yourself totally. What I'm doing can be done by others who are willing to work. It's all out there.

Another thing is that even though I'm still in pre-Med and doing fine, I'm not maniacally concerned with grades. You have to enjoy yourself. Especially around here. Also, I like to keep in shape and work out at least an hour every day. Since I've stopped playing basketball I've taken up karate, and I'm a first-degree black belt. I enjoy that and am very active in it.

GAME PLAN   To Be a Portfolio Manager

A. Market: People interested in investing.

   1. Approach: Free information is offered to potential clients to gain their confidence and cash.
   2. Price: The total number of fund dollars will be kept around $100,000 for now, possible expansion later.
   3. Timing: A day-to-day (sometimes an hour-to-hour) approach to buying stock is advocated.

B. Competition: The high rate of return on money invested leaves other investors far behind.

C. Goods and Overhead

   1. Materials: Graphs, annual reports, research, and a telephone.

D. Capital: This operation involved not a cent in start-up costs, nor does it require any more than nominal expenses to continue.

E. Regulations: The Securities and Exchange Commission laws govern all transactions.

F. Risk

    1. Financial: Nothing to lose except credibility.

G. Time Commitment: Daily scrutiny of the following data: financial reports, market data, market trends, current events, and corporate news, which must be observed to play the stock market intelligently.

H. What's Involved

    1. Obtaining funds to manage.

    2. Successfully investing the funds.

Clearly, Jim Carona is an impressive guy. But his method can be used by anyone else. As he put it, "What I'm doing can be done by others who are willing to work. It's all out there." At the heart of his method is the theory of one man (Joseph Granville), but there are plenty of other theories out there in addition to Granville's. All it takes, as Carona said, is a lot of research and hard work. You don't have to be in a special area of the country. All the exchanges are available to anyone with a telephone and access to a computer terminal or, failing that, a daily newspaper. The stock exchanges on the East Coast aren't the only ones in the country by far. There are commodities exchanges and futures exchanges and just about any other kind you can name, from Chicago to San Francisco. What Carona is really teaching is faith in oneself. We hope you notice how often that's been coming up.

Image Presentations: *Mark Edwards*

The first year, when we were in school, we probably grossed only about $75,000. I guess that sounds funny, but I mean it in comparison with what we are doing now.

— *Mark Edwards*

Many freshmen, over the years, have left Harvard after that first year. Most do so because they are looking for something more satisfying. In Mark's case, he had no complaints about the school or his education, but he left because he was so deeply involved in a business he'd started as a high school senior that he couldn't do both. A year later, he was back in school, and the business was still in business. In fact, it was doing better than ever.

A twenty-one-year-old junior from New York City, Mark Edwards is majoring in Government, but his avocation seems closer and closer to becoming his vocation. That avocation is the film production business.

I became interested in film production when I was in high school, at Phillips Exeter Academy. I took some film courses there, at an amateurish, Super-8 level. During my senior year, Exeter decided to have a documentary film made for its bicentennial because Phillips Andover had had one done for its bicentennial a couple of years earlier. The school budgeted $100,000 for the film, which it planned to show the alumni.

Our film teacher knew a former student — Jonathan Spring, now my associate — who was at MIT and was qualified to make the film. Jonathan was hired; when he came up to do the film, I started to help him out because I was in the film class.

We worked in 16-millimeter, a relatively professional medium, and we edited the film together during the summer. Exeter liked it very much.

The following year, when I was a freshman at Harvard and Jonathan a senior at MIT, writing his thesis, other schools began to hear about our work through word of mouth. Prep schools and colleges were interested in our kind of service. MIT, Tabor Academy, Wilson, Northampton Academy. Places like that. They wanted films to show to alumni for fund-raising purposes and for their admissions offices to use in recruiting. We were hired to make several films.

We were squeezing in these jobs between classes. It was a lot of work. It really was. But it was very exciting because we got to travel, and people liked the style of our films.

Then Jonathan graduated; he had been an engineering major but ended up majoring in history of science. I had taken some film courses at MIT my freshman year because they have an excellent film department, and he had been involved with that program as well.

The following summer we made a film for the Marine Biological Laboratory, a scientific institution in Woods Hole, Massachusetts, which was one of our first really large projects. I guess we were paid about $50,000. And it was just the two of us doing it; it's been just the two of us from the beginning, doing everything.

We then decided that I would take the next year off from school, and that he would join me, to try to make a business out of what we were doing, instead of being two college kids working on the side. It had been a crazy time. I'll never forget the time I was in New York City, where we had done a film for the Hospital for Special Surgery, and we were asked to show it at a big benefit. The "opening" for the film was a big, formal lunch, and a lot of celebrities who had been patients in the hospital showed up — Tom Brokaw narrated the film; Arthur Ashe was there; so was Mayor Koch. It was a big deal. I guess the luncheon was over about four, and I had to catch the five o'clock shuttle to Boston so I could make my seven o'clock tutorial. I was hoping someone would say, "And what was your day like?"

We were already making what we considered to be

good money. The first year, when we were in school and grossed about $75,000, we were working out of Jonathan's apartment and my dorm room, which was not quite kosher.

We set up a place in Boston, on the top floor of a brownstone. At first we called our company "CV Films," for cinema verité, but later changed it to "Image Presentations." We had projects lined up, based on what we had already done, and started working on those, plus putting together some more sophisticated brochure materials.

We continued for a while working just for schools, making both films and multiprojector slide shows — six projectors on one screen, that kind of thing, with a computer running it, and music and sound. But at the end of that year we began to see that there was a lot of work to be had, a large market, in corporations. Doing presentations for sales meetings. For example, we did one show for Gillette. They were introducing a new product, and they flew their sales force to Boston to have a big meeting about it and get all excited about it, and we put on an audiovisual presentation to get them all worked up.

We started doing more of that kind of work. The best part was that all of our new business was from people who had seen our earlier work and liked it. We weren't using any "Harvard contacts," or anything like that. We were indeed making it in the real world, as it were. And we never advertised.

It was a difficult year; we didn't always have as much work as we wanted, so there were some long, long moments when we worried. I'd always thought of myself as a straight-through-college guy — go four years, graduate, get a job, and do whatever. Yet there I was, taking this year off; I didn't know what I was doing, and we weren't raking it in.

Now most parents would not exactly like to have their son at Harvard take his second year off, but fortunately my parents were very good about it. They were very understanding.

By the end of the year jobs had begun to come in, and we began to get busy in production. Things began to pick up by June, which was almost a year from the time we started, using an academic calendar. We had spent a lot of time writing brochures, and the whole previous summer had been pretty much taken up with the Marine Biological Lab's film. By the nine-month point we were actually doing pretty well.

By June of 1980, we were fine, getting both school and corporate jobs. People in the Boston area saw our stuff because our films were being shown all around, which led to new contracts and expanded office space. We still hadn't hired a secretary, but we did have furniture and all of that. Then, just as things were really beginning to take off, I had to go back to school.

I had made the decision earlier that I was going to finish school. But in the back of my mind there had been some doubt as to whether or not I would. I was doing exactly what I wanted to do, with people I wanted to do it with. After a year, all our hard labor had really paid off, but there I was, back in school, writing papers and such.

That first year back was really difficult for me because we had clients who called us and expected us to be in certain places at certain times. Working in the corporate sector was much more fast-paced than working for schools. Schools were usually interested in having all the seasons shown in their film, so there was no rush. But somebody in a corporation would say, "We have to have this twelve-projector show in a month, okay?" Also, corporate executives would say, "Here's all the money you need," which was great, but there was still the deadline problem. It was not easy, trying to balance the work and the academics.

People hire us for the quality of our work, which, by the way, includes everything from script to screen. A lot of people make slide shows and films, but our clients like the way we do them. One of the things I find most satisfying is that even corporate clients give us a lot of leeway. We are rarely handed a script and told what to do.

Of course, that necessitates a great deal of research. When we did a film for IBM on lasers, we had to learn all about them first. That took a considerable amount of work. One of the most gratifying things for me is getting the chance to learn about so many different areas in a short amount of time. For instance, the summer we did the film for the Marine Biological Laboratory I learned more about what was going on in science than in all my years of schooling in biology and chemistry classes put together. The show we did on lasers was the same kind of thing. I find that very, very exciting.

After that second summer we hired a secretary and were getting a lot of business. When we started doing more corporate work we found that people expected a much more sophisticated kind of show, so we began to tie into a lot of people who were kind of a support staff. For instance, many companies asked us to compose original music for these slide shows, so we got to know composers, and worked with designers who did a lot of the art. Once we got into the corporate market, the scripts got longer and more complicated, the shows themselves got larger, and the deadlines got shorter.

Even though I'm back in school, we haven't had to cut back on those corporate jobs. We now have a sort of repertory company that includes producers, photographers, and designers; Jonathan and I are able to keep creative control of what goes on in these projects. We act much more as managers. In our first years, we would do *everything* ourselves, from going out and getting the batteries when our flashes were dead, to writing the script, to client contact. Now, I think what we do most is write scripts. But I enjoy writing scripts.

We have kept the office small on purpose. Only three of us work full time — Jonathan, the secretary, and I, even though I'm not really there full time. In addition, we have five or six people who regularly work with us on projects. I think that our gross, the company's gross, is probably around $250,000 a year.

Right now it looks as though I'll stay with this work after graduation. At one point Jonathan and I hoped to go to Hollywood to make feature films, but I think my goal's a little more shortsighted. I really enjoy what we are doing now.

People who would like to get into this business might like to know that we started out by renting our equipment, but as we got more jobs we slowly built up a good base of equipment; now we have a full studio with full mixing facilities.

We keep our overhead very low, and originally that was very good because we could undersell our local competition. Now I think we charge the same as everyone else, so I think that worked out very well.

From very early on, even though I didn't exhibit an entrepreneurial bent, I still had a very strong desire to work for myself. What's more, in school I was often the business-manager type who helped run things.

I want to repeat and stress that I don't think what we did is or would be at all impossible or even very hard to duplicate, or to do on a smaller scale, perhaps. We started with no capital at all. However, later, and unlike many other small businesses, we never had to get a loan to buy equipment or for any other purpose. Like any other art form, making films or slide shows does involve some sort of — I hate to use the word *talent* — but maybe *creativity* is a better word.

On the other hand, when you look at the way we started, there was nothing very special about what we had. We didn't have any great connections or great amounts of equipment; we were just students. I think that our success was just a function of being able to work really hard. Also, I learned with a used Kodak camera and Super-8 film, which is not at all expensive or hard to get.

It takes a long time to learn filmmaking, but anyone who's done it will tell you that it is worthwhile because it is so enjoyable. Other than a willingness to work hard, I don't think there's anything magic, or anything lucky. I just think it takes desire. It meant so much to us to make the thing work that it wasn't like work.

Those who want to start may well do just what we did — make a film about something you know, like your school. Films about schools, which can be used for recruiting or fund-raising or for alumni events, are much more common now. Everybody's fighting for the same students or the same money, and an attractive, interesting film can put one school ahead. That's a good place to start.

GAME PLAN   To Create Film Productions

A. Market: Corporations and schools.

1. Approach: Start small, working with a school or familiar material, then expand through exposure gained.

2. Price: Originally they charged less than the going market price for similar services to gain access to this competitive industry; now their prices mirror competitors'.

3. Timing: Corporations demand a concentrated effort by imposing short deadlines, while schools usually require a spectrum of seasonal events.

B. Competition: This is a highly competitive industry.

C. Goods and Overhead

1. Materials: Film needed for production and brochures to be used in soliciting work. Under $400.

2. Equipment: Initially, equipment was rented as needed; now the equipment is in-house.

3. Facilities: Office and production space. ($500 per month for 800 square feet.)

D. Capital: Required no start-up capital; later, profit went toward expansion and for equipment.

1. Cash flow: Slower from schools than from corporations.

E. Risk

1. Financial: No risk because of zero capitalization.

F. Time Commitment: Full-time attention must be given for the successful operation of this service, with intermittent periods of lengthy and short working days.

G. What's Involved
    1. Combining the use of a camera and filming equipment with hard work.
    2. Creating a top quality product, which should attract new clients.

Mark Edwards's experience is yet another example of a theme that runs through so many of the ventures described in this book: you don't have to have a lot of money to get started (in lots of instances you don't need any). Think how many kids have taken film classes in high school over the last decade. That represents a lot of opportunities. Remember, Mark and his partner used rental equipment to begin with; they also gave their first customers a price break to make up for their lack of experience and as an incentive to buy. Although Image Presentations didn't do it to any great degree, readers who are interested in this field should spend some time up front studying the different markets they want to pursue or concentrate on. (Look at the differences found by Image Presentations between schools and corporations.) Don't make the mistake of limiting your markets to just these two. Remember Monroe Trout, the basketball player who sells film booklets? He mentioned any number of good uses for film, from taking pictures of household goods for insurance purposes to filming weddings, bar mitzvahs, and other social and religious gatherings. Just aim the camera and go!

Mr. Crowd Caps: *Brett Johnson*

An olive baseball-style cap emblazoned with the trademark of the U.S. Tobacco Company covers Brett Johnson's well-creased brow. A crumbled United States Army Reserve hat protrudes from his bulging book bag. Assorted other hats with the insignias of Southern colleges are stuffed in his back pockets. Perhaps it is not the standard operating procedure for a million dollar a year business, but this senior at Harvard College is not running his company, Crowd Caps, out of the seat of his pants. He's running it out of his college dormitory.

Crowd Caps is one of a dozen infant businesses born on Harvard's campus recently, in a birthrate reminiscent of the student protest movements a decade ago. But unlike many of the now-forgotten political entities, Brett Johnson's company, and several others like it, may last beyond their graduation days.

New York Times
January 17, 1982

James Cramer, the *New York Times* reporter, was correct in beginning his long article about Harvard entrepreneurs with Brett Johnson. Brett was ahead of us, in this "generation," and he fought many of the same fights we fought a few years later. But he was more than willing to share with us his secrets and insights.

A twenty-three-year-old senior from Minneapolis, with a major in Economics, Brett Johnson leaves Harvard with some very special plans.

When I was younger I thought I might make playing competitive golf my career, and in order to do that I had to be able to make money in the summer but still be able to get off for tournaments. So the summer I was fourteen I painted my parents' house, that kind of thing. After my freshman year of college I went back and started a company called Collegiate Driveway Sealcoating Company. Prior to that, my only real entrepreneurial activity had been as a senior in high school, when, for Senior Night,

we rented a gigantic boat and trucked around Lake Min-
netonka with about one hundred couples. That was a
very involved promotion.

When I got to Harvard, I saw that there was a need for
parties, and I wanted to change that, so I decided to start
the Harvard Party Company. It was simply an organization to throw parties. My first party was after the Dart-
mouth football game. I really was going out on a limb,
because I got about fifteen kegs of beer, on credit, hired a
band, on credit, rented the Harvard Union and went
through all the rigamarole getting a license, and pulled it
off. I charged each person $1.50 to get in, made a few
hundred dollars, and started a company to do the business of throwing parties at Harvard. I didn't do this so
much because I needed money, but because I thought it
was an idea that would be worth executing. I wanted to
see if I could pull it off, and it was exciting.

That fall I also sold T-shirts at the Harvard-Yale game.
A friend of mine — who was then the captain of the golf
team and now is a vice president of a New York investment bank and into about six figures — and I commissioned a bunch of T-shirts that said "Impale Yale." We
went to New Haven, where the game was held that year,
and hawked those T-shirts at five bucks a crack. We had
bought about five hundred of them for $2.50 apiece, so
we had a good return on that. In the spring we threw a
few more parties, but the party business wasn't all that
great.

After that year I went back to Minneapolis and started
the Collegiate Driveway Sealcoating Company. That was
just putting the black covering over driveways, which is
an excellent business for any student to get into. In
seven weeks I netted about $2,200. I was on my own
hours, met lots of people, and did about sixty driveways
in about seven weeks. I didn't have to get a license, or
anything like that. I just went out and bought an old
beat-up pickup truck, an old beat-up station wagon, went
down to the sealcoating company over in St. Paul, got a
couple fifty-five-gallon drums of sealcoating, took them
back to my garage, mixed them with water in five-gallon

pails, threw them into the back of the old beat-up station wagon, and went out into the community and started doing driveways.

I did a little advertising by distributing little brochures and making sales calls about dinnertime at houses where I'd seen that the driveways needed to be done and where I'd left a brochure. I charged about $85 or $90, something like that for the average four-car driveway. Reasonable. Real big driveways could bring as high as $250. I did it by myself, except that for some of the bigger driveways I would subcontract some of my friends and pay them $5.00 an hour. It was a good experience, and I made lots of money.

That summer I came across a product that, as things turned out, had a great future. When I sealed the driveways I wore a painter's cap, the kind you buy at the paint store. And I thought, "Gee, these things are great. They're light and they're comfortable." When I came back that fall, I sold painters' caps at the Harvard-Yale football game. White caps with a little red *H* on the front. They went well. I didn't sell all of them, because I was somewhat disorganized and didn't get the caps until the morning of the game, which didn't help anything. But I sold the rest of them at commencement that spring.

Also in the spring, I took a course called "Business in American Life" at the Business School, in which the term project was to identify a business opportunity, or an ongoing business, take a look at its potential, that kind of thing. So I did the hat thing, Crowd Caps — I use the terms interchangeably. I found a manufacturer and checked it all out. Then I said, "Hey, I want to have something when I get out of college, and the hardest part of any organization is the start-up phase; if I drop out of school now I could have sixteen to eighteen months to see if I can start a company marketing and selling these hats."

So I hitchhiked to see the manufacturer in Wisconsin and told him I was going into the hat business; he said fine, and gave me an exclusive on some designs I'd come up with that were an improvement on his company's painter's cap concept, and I was off and running. (My improved version of the painter's cap is what we call the Crowd Cap.)

I came back to the East Coast and did a *wide* range of studies on markets and logos and licensing. I made a lot of mistakes initially. I was out of school and in the hat business.

I came across a partner, halfway through that summer of my first full year out, and the rest has been history. We added a third partner last summer, and recently a fourth. I've given them all small portions of equity in the organization. While I'm at school the company is sort of running itself. And it's doing quite wonderfully.

We started out on the bottom two floors of my parents' home, but we've since moved to downtown Minneapolis; we're in a joint partnership with a manufacturing firm there that makes these kinds of caps, and now we're doing all their marketing. They're doing all our manufacturing, so we really have good quality control. We've doubled the size of the manufacturing arm. It has eighty-nine employees now, up from forty-four. Forty-five hard-core manufacturing jobs have been created by Crowd Caps in the nine months since we joined them. Plus about ten jobs in related areas. Our own company has four partners now, and five employees.

This year we did a half million in sales in the first quarter, and we should do a little bit over two million in sales for the year.

It all started because I came across that little cap and said, "Hey, I could make this thing better and make it retailable." I improved the quality and the logos; it was just a simple innovation. That's the American way — improve it, just make it a little better.

We want to try to build this company up to about $10 million in sales in our various markets. The diversity of the applications of the product and its markets provides an opportunity to build a large marketing and distribution system, into which we can plug other product innovations we are presently developing. I'm working on that right now.

After graduation I will go back to work on the company full time, and we will be opening a West Coast division. I'll be doing that with several other graduating seniors, including Kulu Padua, who is one of the most technically sound people here and a very bright guy.

One of my original ideas in leaving Harvard to get the company going was that I felt that if I could come back, having done something, I could probably succeed in attracting some other very talented people, who were doing complementary things. And then, of course, I came back because I really like Harvard.

The idea was that when I finished I would have a business going and growing, to be up and rolling and really ready to go big time, which is identified by $10-million markets, and it worked out as planned. The company *did* go, I came back, and I think I have attracted three of the most talented graduates this year. The four of us, after an internship period in Minneapolis, will open a West Coast division for Crowd Caps.

Brett Johnson has a very specific plan as to what he will do with the success, present and especially future, of Crowd Caps, and it is behind his planned move to the West Coast and part and parcel of his adding three very bright Harvard classmates to his roster. But before going on to his discussion of that plan, it might be helpful if you met one of the main players in that plan, Kulu Padua.

A twenty-one-year old senior, Kulu is a Biology major who had planned to be a doctor, but that was before he discovered, or would admit, how talented he is in several other areas. In fact, Kulu Padua is a hero, a kind of legend in his own time (like Brett Johnson) to many of us on campus. His skill with computers is amazing; last year he invented a process that would open whole new dimensions for Atari video games, at the same time proving his ability at another type of game, the stock market. Finally, he has published several articles on computer technology in scientific journals.

Of Kulu, Brett Johnson says, "I was very pleased to hear that people are impressed by the fact that Kulu is going to work with me. His ability and aptitude in the hard sciences are amazing, and he has a whole technical dimension that I don't have. I bring a very good marketing dimension to his skills, so we're complementary. If someone brought me a scientific proposal that I couldn't fully understand, he would be able to evaluate it in a second. He had a major article on comparative economic environments of states published in *INC.* magazine last summer. He fully computerized their operation. He's also a computer consultant, so he will be doing some of that for us too."

In all, a pretty amazing guy.

Kulu Padua. My parents are from India, but I grew up in the Virgin Islands, among families with really tough backgrounds. I came out of there with real skepticism toward the corporate world, almost like a knight riding out in shining armor to do battle with that world. But I found out that the best way to win is to end up being able to do things in the world while still being able to work for yourself.

Fairly or unfairly, I still have a lot of bitterness, especially toward two companies, because they just basically took as much as they could from the islands and did absolutely nothing for anyone who worked for them.

It's not fair to attribute that sort of behavior to the entire *Fortune* 500 set, but the human mind is an irrational thing. Because of that background, when I came to Harvard my first impulse was to go into medicine, an area where I'd have independence. On Saint Croix people have no concept of what a high-tech company is.

Once I got up here, after my junior year, I worked for *INC.* magazine. I just walked into their offices, basically, because I'd met one or two of their people here. I was a nineteen-year-old who said I wanted a job, and they said, "What can you do?" So I gave them my whole background

— biology, computers, economics, and all that stuff. They were hesitant to take me on, but they did. What I did for them was a special report, which was an analysis of the business climates for small businesses — high-tech companies — in each of the states. It took me about two months. It was a great two months. Traveling all over the United States gave me a chance to meet small-business people all over the country. It was also exciting because it was the first time I realized the breadth and the scope of the words *small business.*

I chose computer software because it is a very low-barrier entry field. All you have to do, basically, is be able to run a computer.

I am going to Minnesota with Brett Johnson to help him with Crowd Caps. Then we're going to San Diego, to start up another Crowd Caps–type organization, because California and the West Coast market haven't been explored.

When we get to San Diego, we're going to try to start a free service for small businesses. I won't lie — making money is part of the whole thing, certainly; no one wants to live in poverty. But, underlying my motive there is definitely a theme of guilt or responsibility. I mean, if you were one of the have-nots of Saint Croix, you should do your part to help people in a position like yours.

One thing I want to do in San Diego is start this free computer consulting service for small businesses in urban revitalization zones, throughout the entire minority populations — with low skills, no jobs, they're struggling. I hope my advice will make them more competitive — say, open up computerization that could put them in contact with world markets so they can export to other parts of the world, which small businesses are not doing at present.

The federal government is not helping minorities right now, and the big corporations are not doing it either. Everyone is screwing us, so to speak. Small business is one of the only hopes because it is labor-intensive, and thus creates more jobs for every dollar spent. It is a really effective tool for increasing employment.

Earlier this year I had a job offer for big bucks from a company in San Diego that makes precision instruments for airplanes; they wanted someone to oversee the computerization of their entire manufacturing setup. The job would have started off at $31,000 and in a couple of years gone to $35,000. That would have meant hanging out in California and making big bucks, which a lot of people would love to do. But there are so many ways of making money in this world that that can't be your sole motivating factor. At least it's not for me. Because if you're good and you like what you're doing, you'll make money no matter what.

I see this work as more of a tool, a constructive way of bringing about change, rather than sitting outside buildings yelling and screaming, which never accomplishes a thing.

I think that much of the motivation behind the entrepreneurial types is a need for money to help defray expenses. In my case I was able to pay my tuition by making money on the stock market, which isn't exactly entrepreneurial, but it's pretty unusual. If you think about it, it's really unfortunate to have to put all that effort into a $4.00-an-hour job when it could go into something lucrative.

The entrepreneurial venture I've been in is the stock market idea. Basically, what I did was I snuck into a very large computer system — guess whose — sort of cheating to do so, and used this humongous computer, which would have been very expensive if I'd had to rent the time. I put all the data I needed into it: market indicators that had validity plus the ones that are disclaimed, and so on, just fed them in, and I wrote a program for the computer to play with all these factors to see which one of them came closest to the actual Dow-Jones performance that month.

I got about a 75 percent correlation, which is not great but is better than an even bet. And that has worked. Unfortunately, I'm not able to use it that much because I don't have any money to put into it, but I ran it for some friends the end of my sophomore year and we all made some money.

Another idea I had was for a system that would allow expanded memory space on Atari video game cartridges. Those Atari games are really boring; within five minutes any Neanderthal is certainly bored, right? The games are not very complex, and their designers assume the basic fallacy, I think, that the whole program has to be recursive, kind of repeat on itself.

I designed a hardware hookup that can be plugged into the box and attached to a cassette recorder on which you record a new program. The reason that's advantageous is that the cassette could be made and sold much more cheaply. An Atari cartridge might cost $40, but this cassette could sell for $5.00.

There are drawbacks to it, but they are not serious, not with all the graphics available in the machine itself, which it seems to me wastes the use of the memory.

The idea is to use the cassette as a supplement to the cartridges. Because of the limited space, you can only have about 4K — or now, 8K — on an Atari cartridge, and I'm saying that the 8K space is not being used very efficiently. Because that 8K of computer space, which you can play around with to move information, is being used as dead space. The cartridge runs through the program once and that's it.

The point is that you could make a much more interesting game for a much cheaper price. I thought it was a good idea and showed it to a lot of the Harvard people; they also thought it was a good idea and would work, so I went to talk to the Atari people.

Now the problem is that for my innovation to work, for it to hook into the cartridge, I would have to get a code from Atari. When I talked to them I tried to put it on the basis that this idea would increase their sales — in addition to making the game more interesting. But the guy I talked to, who was in Research and Development, took me aside and said, "Look, kid, your idea may work, and it's nice, but we're not going to use it because we're making too much money right now. Once this market's played out, we might consider doing something like that, but, for now, why mess up something that's really going well."

I've been feeling pretty frustrated since then. The only organization that can hook into Atari right now is Activision, which is a company started by former hot-shot Atari people. I may take the idea to them, eventually, but right now I don't have the time. Maybe I'll do it when I get to California with Brett.

Kulu and the other seniors who are going to work with Brett Johnson have a dream that transcends making money. This is the way Brett describes it:

I want to play a role in job creation, specifically starting small businesses. We all feel that way. The idea is to increase the birthrate of companies in America. I'm doing an independent study on unemployment this semester, with Otto Eckstein, and I've found out that there's always going to be a mortality rate — you hear people say that four out of five new businesses fail, but three out of those five are mom-and-pop businesses in somebody's basement. So in part it depends on how you define business start-up. But, historically, the mortality rate is not going to change that much. It's the *birthrate* that is going to change the nature of job creation and unemployment. At least that's what the experts I talked to have told me.

There are real opportunities in this country for the lower and middle classes. One of the things we are excited about, particularly Kulu and I, is the idea of creating job opportunities for people who have previously been unable to go into business for themselves. We want to participate in the private sector, filling the gap, providing opportunities for all Americans, especially those on the bottom, and replacing the government. We want to show that innovative, private free-market entrepreneurship can address some of these social problems. And make money at the same time.

It's the ultimate creative act to bring about wealth and opportunities at the same time. We'd like to think that we could have a substantial positive impact on the future of this country by providing jobs. The best welfare program there ever was is a job.

GAME PLAN **To Market an Improved Painter's Cap**

A. Market: An open-ended market that will use a relatively low-cost hat as a promotional item.

   1. Approach: Select choice markets, then promote the possibilities to them.

   2. Price: Prices fluctuate, depending on style and quality.

   3. Timing: Year round.

B. Competitors: The exclusivity on certain cap designs provides a unique angle in approaching the market.

C. Goods and Overhead

   1. Materials: Promotional items.

   2. Equipment: The manufacturing is subcontracted.

   3. Facilities: An office for full-time partners and employees.

D. Capital: Very little start-up capital was necessary and expansion has been largely financed through earnings.

E. Risk

   1. Financial: Since orders are usually taken before production begins, the monetary risk is minimal.

F. Time Commitment: The start-up phase involved full-time hard work. The current operation requires full-time attention to expand markets and fill orders.

G. What's Involved

   1. Selecting the product.

   2. Determining the proper markets.

   3. Promoting the product.

   4. Soliciting orders.

   5. Arranging for manufacture.

   6. Distributing the final product.

At one point Brett Johnson makes a comment that all readers should pay close attention to. He says, in reference to the fact that he improved but did not *invent* the caps, that innovation is the American way. He is quite right. Think of how many of our great "inventors," like Henry Ford, were really not inventors at all, but rather very talented and farsighted innovators. For another example from this section, note Kulu's idea for spicing up the Atari game — another innovation. Our point is that you should never be discouraged if your idea is not totally original; the important thing is whether anyone else has thought of your particular angle. Brett also said that before he got too deeply involved with Crowd Caps he "found a manufacturer and checked it all out." This is really easier than it sounds. All it means is that he found a company that made the original painters' hats, told them what he had in mind, and asked how difficult it would be for them to make the hats. Any company that understands you are a serious potential customer will be glad to help you that way. They often know exactly what is around in the way of competition, information that can be a big help to learn sooner rather than later. Never hesitate to ask a question when you truly need to know the answer, even if it seems to be embarrassing. It doesn't pay to be shy.

BOOK FOUR

Entrepreneurism: Passing Fad? or Future?

1
Interviews with Professor Howard Stevenson and "Madame Wellington" (Helen Ver Standig)

Originally, we were going to end this book by giving you our thoughts about the future of entrepreneurism. Then we decided that maybe you'd feel you'd heard enough from us, so we interviewed people who qualify as experts on the subject. We think you'll enjoy "hearing" them as much as we enjoyed interviewing them.

At first glance, the two people may seem to be very different. One is a university professor, and the other runs a highly successful retail business. But a closer look will reveal some interesting similarities. The professor has a long history of working in and with entrepreneurial ventures, and the retailer also teaches a course in entrepreneurism at the University of Pennsylvania's Wharton School of Business. Each, as you will see, is a remarkable person.

Professor Howard Stevenson was recently named Harvard University's first professor of entrepreneurism. Officially, he is the Sarofim-Rock Professor of Business Administration, and as such he is in charge of "teaching and course development relating to the development of general management skills for entrepreneurs." He is on the faculty of the Graduate School of Business Administration for the second time. In addition, Professor Stevenson has held positions in private enterprise and is a director of numerous investment trusts and corporations.

Helen Ver Standig has been a businesswoman for almost forty-five years. She and her late husband owned and operated radio stations and other businesses, including what was for years the largest advertising agency south of New York City. In the late 1960s, she financed the development of a process for making simulated diamonds, which soon turned into the very real Wellington stores, a chain of retail jewelry shops. The firm's logo is an Al Hirshfeld caricature of the now-famous "Madame Wellington" — a diamond-bedecked Mrs. Ver Standig, sporting a long cigarette holder.

Madame Wellington has lectured on entrepreneurism for some years. In 1981 she was given the Joseph Wharton award by the Wharton Club of Washington.

The following is an edited version of our interviews with Professor Stevenson and Mrs. Ver Standig.

Q. How do you define "entrepreneurism," or, put another way, what is an entrepreneur?

A. PROFESSOR STEVENSON: I have a definition, but first let's look at what it isn't. It's *not* risk-taking, because a lot of good entrepreneurs hate risk and will do anything they can to avoid it. It's *not* capitalism. I know a lot of good entrepreneurs who are not the major owners of their companies. And it's *not* free enterprise, because you see entrepreneurs springing up in all sorts of economies. In fact, you can even find people within the government who have what I would have to call an entre-preneurial bent.

So what is it? To me, it is the difference between people who are opportunity-driven and those who are resource-driven. Some people are driven to maximize the resources they control; entrepreneurs are driven to chasing opportunity.

A. MADAME WELLINGTON: I've always said that the true entrepreneur, strangely enough, is the "unemployable." He or she is the nonconformist, the person who doesn't fit the mold. I think of some of my former advertising clients and wonder what it was that made these people leave good, solid jobs and go into business for them-selves. In analyzing these people, including myself, I concluded that it didn't have anything to do with money.

They are human beings who, basically, had to do some-thing on their own. It wasn't that they were really "un-employable," but that somehow they couldn't stay in a mold and climb the corporate structure.

A true entrepreneur can fail *fifty* times, and he'll still go back. It's true in my own case. I had failures when I was young, and so did my husband. We started in the weekly newspaper business and we had financial prob-lems — we once lost a newspaper in Rhode Island, and we damn near lost one in South Carolina. We left South Carolina broke! We worked for a radio station to get going again, and once we got some money together we went right back into business. That's the way it is with entrepreneurs.

Q. Do you think there is an increase in entrepreneurism today?

A. PROFESSOR STEVENSON: I think there's a new recog-nition that the world is not going to end with just one big company, of which Exxon and IBM are minor subsidi-aries. In the 1970s the whole notion was that the world was getting more complex and that the problem was one of administration. I think that now more and more people are recognizing that the problem is maintaining and emphasizing that creative spark which somehow gets around administrative procedures.

A. MADAME WELLINGTON: Sure. Because today young people realize that the General Motors, the Ford Motor Company, the large structure, does not offer this security. Nor does the United States government — which, when I was a kid, promised security if nothing else. Today, in my class at Wharton, I meet vast numbers of kids who say: "I'm going into the perfume business, and I don't care if I have to peddle it door to door as long as it's *mine*."

And look at the franchise business, without getting into whether franchising is good or bad. Look at the people who have made successes in franchising. These are entrepreneurs.

Q. Are more *young* people entrepreneurial?

A. PROFESSOR STEVENSON: Yes, for several reasons. One, young people now have less risk, or perceive themselves to have less risk, so they can afford to take more risk at this point in their lives. Very few young people are worried; they are confident that there will always be a safety net.

A. MADAME WELLINGTON: Young people today are much brighter than they were when I was young. I don't think there's any doubt about that. I think they have learned that most security is a false security.

Q. Do you think that there is an entrepreneurial "type," and an entrepreneurial personality?

A. PROFESSOR STEVENSON: I think that most entrepreneurs are people who want to control their own destiny, but realistically that's not a plausible goal. Once you get the money, for example, you're not necessarily home free. I think most people are reasonably rational about measuring their own opportunities; for example, given a new commission structure, any salesman worth his salt can figure out within two days what games he has to play to maximize it. People understand their own self-interest.

Plenty of studies talk about the need for achievement, but a lot of that is self-fulfilling in the sense that if you measure it by your desire to be independent you can get a lot of circular reasoning.

Or take the difference between the organizational entrepreneur and the independent entrepreneur — the organizational entrepreneur may have ninety-nine out of a hundred people who say yes, but the one who says no can kill the deal, whereas the independent entrepreneur, who may have ninety-nine who say no and one who says yes, can go ahead anyway.

A. MADAME WELLINGTON: I think there is a certain drive, which, if you are honest about it, is almost indefinable.

The guy who is willing to work for his $25,000 or $30,000 a year, or whatever, and is *content,* he isn't hungry. He's not insecure. He thinks he's got it made; he's going to get his check every week. But, as a good example, when I was in the advertising business — and my husband and I were in it for thirty years — out of a staff of over a hundred, the best employees were the men who wanted to steal everything we had. They made a lot of money for us, but when they left they were successful in their own agencies. They were the greatest because they were hungry.

Q. What motivates the entrepreneur?

A. PROFESSOR STEVENSON: It certainly isn't money alone. A high percentage of the people I teach will end up with their own businesses, but for a lot of reasons other than money. At a certain point, money becomes a rather irrelevant measure of your life. I know very few people who have succeeded as entrepreneurs who were motivated primarily by money. I think most were motivated by other things, such as independence, power, or just trying to do a better job at something.

I know very few people who can keep going just for the money. Now, you can accumulate money, but at a certain point you have to ask yourself, "How many cars, or houses, do I want?" And you soon run out of answers to that question.

I think that, on a political basis, that's one of the healthy things about capitalism. Money is a satiating quantity.

A. MADAME WELLINGTON: The people I lecture to at Wharton want to go out and start their own businesses. They're willing to start for less. It's like grabbing the brass ring. I don't think that money is the motivating factor for them. I think the motivating factor is the sense of independence.

Motivating factors are very interesting. Years ago, when I was in advertising, we did a lot of marketing research, and once we were paid a huge retainer, $200,000, I think, to find out how one could woo engineers away from a big outfit like, say, Westinghouse. We, of course, assumed that money would do it, an additional $10,000 and a down payment on a house. But it turned out that what the engineers really moved for was the project! Or self-esteem, and such things as the cultural activities available to them and their families. It had *nothing* to do with money.

People say it takes so much courage to become an entrepreneur. I think it takes far more courage to work for somebody else, to get up each morning and go to work and not have something in your control. And you can get canned! That would drive me up a wall.

Q. What's the role of the business school, graduate or undergraduate, in turning out entrepreneurs? How are they doing today?

A. PROFESSOR STEVENSON: I think business school is the greatest way to get a set of very powerful tools. I'm a chauvinist for business schools — this is my third time here so I should be. I think that we really have an important mission. All the courses here deal with three questions: Where am I? Where do I want to be? How do I bridge the gap? And that's true of life, of business, and of society. We give people the tools to answer those questions, especially "Where do I want to be?"

A. MADAME WELLINGTON: I think the schools have done a good job — Wharton, with its entrepreneurial studies, Harvard, Babson, and Stanford. The universities themselves have done a good job, but that's only in the last ten years or so. I have to assume that eventually this will be good for the economy.

Q. Is it the idea of entrepreneurism or the actuality of being in business for oneself that interests you?

A. PROFESSOR STEVENSON: I've always thought that business was one of the most exciting things around, for the very simple reason that it is the last outpost of the Renaissance person.

I know of no other field where I need to know as much of the world and all its dimensions in order to be successful as I do as an entrepreneur. And that's exciting to me personally.

I don't, however, feel that way about going to work for a lot of companies. You couldn't *sentence* me to that. I would rather dig ditches.

A. MADAME WELLINGTON: Somebody from a big magazine once asked me why I was in business for myself, and I said, "Because I can steal from petty cash!" And I mean it. If I worked for somebody else I would be up for larceny. I'm in business for myself because I can write it off!

Whatever I have is mine. I'm totally responsible for my success and I'm totally responsible for my failure.

When I teach a class at Wharton, after a three-hour session I can pick out the eight or ten who will not make it on their own. I can tell that something is missing. You see, it's something *inside* a person. If you have it, you can take it anywhere.

BOOK FIVE

Getting Down to Business

1

Guide to
First-Time Ventures

A smart entrepreneur recognizes the complexity of the business world. Indeed, a number of essential components are inherent in the formation and maintenance of all business ventures. We hope the following will provide some insights and trigger creative thinking about how to apply these general guidelines to your specific business needs.

Management

Management is by far the most important facet of any business. Good management may take a poor idea and fair capitalization and make it go; but with poor management the most wonderful idea will flounder despite ample capitalization. In fact investors often base their predictions of the potential of an enterprise on the strengths of the management team. The thoroughness of a produced business plan as well as recommendations from associates can lend clues as to the quality of the manager.

The wise entrepreneur may ask his potential investors to make suggestions regarding management, since investors may have preferences or know managers with good track records. Their experience in evaluating personnel can prove invaluable. Attracting management for first-time ventures is complicated by the risky nature of a start-up, and by the fact that scarcity of cash usually means salaries below market value, thus, the entrepreneur must entice management by offering one or more of the following: equity options; royalties; a good deal of freedom; a promise that management will sacrifice its own immediate compensation until the project is solvent.

Remember:

- select lean and hungry management
- set up incentives to encourage results
- do not offer jobs to friends or relatives who have no experience or expertise
- establish one leader in the office; too many chiefs spoil the plan
- go after top management people, perhaps giving up greater equity to attract them
- hire only when absolutely necessary
- establish job responsibilities from the start to avoid future disputes and confusion

Professionals

Numerous individuals who are not original members of a business can, however, provide necessary services and functions. In fact, these people often have tremendous influence on a business, and may offer information or perform services that the entrepreneur needs. Choose these individuals seriously and carefully. Before employing anyone, check their credentials thoroughly. Learning not to underestimate the influence and impact professionals will have on a venture can be a hard lesson.

As with anyone who is being paid for his or her services, these individuals can be compensated in a variety of ways, including payments, equity, merchandise, or cash. Innovative compensation packages designed to attract talented support personnel may be critical in the venture's early stages. In almost all cases, the rates they charge are negotiable, so be ready to bargain.

Lawyers — Virtually any operation, from board of directors meetings to patents, in some way requires legal aid. For an ambitious entrepreneur, finding a competent, hard-working lawyer should be a priority. Do not overlook smaller firms; they will often provide greater flexibility and support than a large, prestigious firm.

Accountants — These individuals prepare financial statements that are presented to investors and Uncle Sam. Again, seek some recommendations before choosing.

Consultants — Keep a shovel around when dealing with many of them. A poor consultant is a waste of time and money, so seek references before hiring. A consultant with a good reputation may be worth his weight in gold when approaching investors or advising in his area of specialty. However, since consultants are not full-time employees, the construction of an incentive program is particularly important.

Production

Assembling a product efficiently means that the final cost will stand up under the pressures of the market. In other words, it will be competitive. Historically, companies that allow production workers to share in the benefits of increased productivity provide incentives for all employees to maximize output.

Production strategy should involve a variety of factors. For example, the degree of quality — how good the product is — should be neither above nor below what the market will support. However, the $5.00 determined quality level should be consistent with the control system introduced at the beginning of production, and carefully groomed as production capacity increases. Factors such as the cost of transportation, sources of raw materials, and potential labor disputes must also be considered.

Remember:

- use a carrot, not a stick, to increase productivity
- reward behavior that strengthens the company
- keep abreast of technological advances
- occasionally take moderate risks; they may lessen profits temporarily, but will strengthen the viability of the company
- subcontracting may increase production
- joint ventures in research and development with a complementary product may be used to improve production and increase demand

Marketing

Determining the market may involve sampling the population. Once the market has been selected, targeting the sales effort in a manner that will yield business involves knowledge of the market's social, political, and economic behavior. To understand the behavior of the market, one must learn its buying patterns, beliefs, and attitudes before setting a course on a sales program. Depending on your product, sampling techniques range from door to door questioning to consultation with your local chamber of commerce. Don't underestimate the support "Uncle Sam" can provide.

The cost of reaching your audience should be weighed in relation to the percentage of the market that will actually purchase the goods. Also, when entering a new market, it is important to analyze the existing competition and to consider the potential for new or future competitors. Find out in advance whether the related goods and services you will be relying on will continue to be available.

Remember:

- pay careful attention to potential competitors when evaluating the market
- whenever possible, test-market the product or service on a limited basis first
- plan strategies in advance to compensate for the market's behavior
- improve a marketing plan even if it's working
- an idle marketer invites competition

Advertising

Advertising should inform, persuade, or reinforce beliefs, attitudes, and behavior. Effective advertising demands a thorough understanding of the nature of the targeted market. Dollars invested wisely in promotion or free publicity through promotional activities often provide the impetus needed to launch or save a venture.

Remember:

- focus advertising on the targeted market
- repeat advertising is generally more effective than one-time ads
- flyers, direct mail, posters, bulletin boards, newspapers, magazines, television, billboards, imprinted clothing, and bumper stickers frequently serve as means of reaching the desired audience

- licensing arrangements for brand endorsement, sponsoring an event, or planning a publicity stunt can provide more exotic forms of advertising
- the mode of advertising can take many forms, but finding cost-effective means requires analyzing information from a variety of advertising campaigns and other sources
- one must invest money to make money; advertising epitomizes this slogan

Salespeople

The sales force is often key to the success of a venture. Attracting competent salespeople means providing incentives that will foster excitement and encourage dedication.

Remember:

- offer incentives tied to performance
- educate salespeople about the nature of the business to develop their loyalty and a sense of pride in the product
- fire salespeople who don't adequately represent the image of the product and company; though they may generate cash flow in the short run, they can do long-term damage
- require professionalism at all times because your salespeople *are* the company in the minds of the customer

Short Tips

Distribution — Establish a network to deliver a product or service to a stated destination. In instances where the goods or services are time-sensitive, planning an effective and reliable means of transportation demands careful analysis. Consider the risks of missing a deadline, and establish an alternative plan in case a crisis should arise. With non-time-sensitive items, costs should be kept to a minimum. Various means of distribution may range from foot to satellite. Discovering the numerous ways to find a favorable price reduces costs.

Name — The name should say something about the product or service that will aid in the marketing. A name can be a nonsense syllable that, through association or advertising, takes on a meaning or evokes an emotional response conducive to encouraging market movement.

Cash Flow — Cash is king. A company can survive even though it is losing money if it can maintain cash flow. Large corporations float millions of dollars a day, collecting interest and, in effect, borrowing it. Creditors often take a back seat when a company's cash reserves become low, just as in the case of foreign debts, because a company without cash often ends up in Chapter 11 — bankruptcy. When cash becomes tight, close the checkbook. By the same token, know the financial condition of your customers and demand cash from those that are too risky.

Novel Idea or a Better Mousetrap — Opportunities exist! Before arriving at any solution, look at and assess everything. Many people may be exposed to the same opportunity, but few can recognize it and capitalize on it.

Being an entrepreneur is an internal state. The difficulty comes in externalizing the insights that later result in a new product or an improved service that may have had a market which no one else saw or could capture.

Legal Structures — Deciding which legal form best suits a particular venture depends on the specific tax advantages, the liability, and the desired ease of investment.

Raising Money

Money should be viewed as one aspect of business with a cost of its own. Thus, raising money involves shopping around for the best deal. Sophisticated investors usually require a business plan from anyone seeking funds, so we have included a description of a business plan in the following section.

Remember:

- numerous sources of money exist, such as families, banks, and venture capitalists
- approach investors who have deeper pockets than just the funds required (in case trouble arises)
- offer investors equity in the new company or leverage on existing assets to obtain funds
- ask for the total amount of projected money required; do not undercapitalize
- consider "worst-case scenarios" when raising funds
- try to attract investors who can provide expertise or in some way bring more than money to the party

Last words of advice: Approach the venture with 100 percent commitment and 110 degrees of energy. Keep the dream alive!

2
Creating a
Business Plan

Business plans are constructed for two primary purposes. First, they are designed to provide an operational framework that will serve as a foundation upon which to build a company. The hours of thought applied to constructing a comprehensive business plan result in the company's being able to anticipate future problems and ways to circumvent them. Second, a business plan often serves to attract the funds necessary to begin a company and support it in its formative stages. Since the business plan is designed to guide a company, its content can be fairly interpreted by potential investors as indicative of the company's thoughtfulness, thoroughness, and insight.

A business plan should never be viewed as a finished product. Constant revisions indicate a progressive company, one learning and adapting to its environment. However, the focus and direction that the business intends to follow should be fairly consistent, particularly if the document has been shown to potential investors. A company that cannot decide what its major project is will not find it easy to attract funding.

It would be valuable to begin creating your first business plan before committing yourself to a venture. The questions that must be addressed will force a more objective view of the venture's potential for success. Most entrepreneurs mentally create some type of business plan before even considering an idea. We would advocate committing such plans to paper. Such a document can often be used to solicit criticism from knowledgeable outsiders whose advice can help you avoid some of the inevitable pitfalls associated with beginning a company. We did not begin our first business plan until four months after forming Fuel Tech. Would that we had!

The business plan should include these key sections:

Summary Profile. Provide a summary analysis of the company. Since many of the people to whom you may wish to send your plan probably receive a great many such plans, it is very important to make this section exciting.

History. A *brief* summary of the company's background. Outline the roles that the primary officers played in the company's establishment. If funds have been raised, a listing of who contributed what amounts when should be included.

Description of the Business. Identify your company's "vital organs." Describe the product or service that you plan to offer, and the characteristics that will distinguish it in the marketplace. Any objective analyses that support your feelings, whether they are gleaned from periodicals, Department of Commerce figures, or market surveys, should be added here. It is also important to consider the flaws in your product and possible ways to eliminate them or obviate weaknesses caused by them. No one will believe that your product has no flaws, so be honest about them; not only is this fact, but it gives you credibility.

Pricing. Indicate what your prices will be, how you have arrived at them, and why you expect that they will enable you to secure a given market share. Do not choose a pricing structure that is designed to provide minimal profit based on precise developmental costs. Many entrepreneurs underestimate their future expenses and the length of time necessary for development and thus set very low prices. Do not undervalue your product.

Industry. Use sources like the Department of Commerce to determine your total market, then define your place in it. A precise focus is crucial; do not overestimate your immediate capabilities, but outline your potential.

Sales Philosophy. What factors did you consider in determining your specific market? How do you plan to enter your market? Better sales techniques? What are they? Quality? What specific characteristics? Do people care? How do you know? Pricing: if your product will be less expensive, why? Can production keep pace with a successful sales program?

Competition. Do not underestimate your competition. Think this section through particularly well, outlining specific competitive companies and products, perhaps using charts to compare their products and services with yours. You should also attempt to determine other factors that could affect your performance negatively, such as social fads or regulatory changes.

Facilities and Equipment. Briefly outline your company's production facilities, as well as the strengths and weaknesses of your equipment. If you foresee having to expand or acquire new machinery, explain what factors will influence these decisions.

Organization. Introduce all the principals in this section. If you are using the business plan to solicit funds, it may be a good idea to get various qualified individuals to agree contractually to join the organization as funding is gained. Also include a description of the company's capital structure, and any agreements to which the company is subject.

Elements of Risk. This section is designed to highlight the risks that the company foresees and the steps it is taking to reduce or eliminate them. The ability to anticipate risks, and take steps to circumvent them, is clearly a quality that is valuable and necessary. Be particularly thoughtful about this section.

Business Plan. Highlight the assumptions on which the company's fundamental analysis is constructed. Usually outlined in three twelve-month periods, the company's plan of action in order to reach its objectives is the final section of this business plan.

This is our rudimentary guide to the construction of a business plan. More complete guides can be found in most large bookstores and business school libraries. You must realize that the construction of a plan varies with its potential use and the product it is outlining. At any rate, the time required for the mental gymnastics necessary to write such a plan should result in a valuable document.

Good luck!

3

A Last Word —
Of Encouragement

You have now met all the people we wanted you to meet, and you have heard all we have to say. At least you have heard *almost* all we have to say. We want to reemphasize something we said at the very beginning, something we hope has become clearer to you as you read through each section, and that is that *YOU* can do it! You can do the things you have just read about.

We're not saying that you can or should do *exactly* as the people we've included in this book have done. That wouldn't be creative, and creativity is one of the distinguishing characteristics of an entrepreneur. What we are saying is that you can start your own version of any of these ventures *as long as you believe you can do it and are willing to work hard.*

Your slant on an idea like Mark Edwards's Image Presentations may be slightly different. That's fine. Or you may take Juggles's act on the road and make it a traveling-minstrel attraction. Or you might like to sell Eskimo, instead of South Seas, jewelry. All that's fine too. Remember, this country is famous for "reinventing the wheel." There is nothing wrong with adapting another's idea to your own special circumstances, and there is absolutely nothing wrong with improving on it. If you didn't take the idea and make it a little better, we'd be disappointed in you.

Also, don't make the mistake of thinking that you have to go to Harvard to take advantage of these ideas. True, there is only one Harvard, which is why we came here in the first place. But Harvard doesn't have an exclusive franchise on talent or energy or productivity. And no school — whether a high school or a college or a university — gives you a *guarantee* along with your diploma. You, your talent and ability and what you do with them — that's what counts.

Finally, don't let others discourage you from going out on your own. Energy sets off sparks, and sparks scare some people. But being scared is no reason to keep from acting. Don't be afraid of being different, if you truly believe in the worth of what you want to do.

We've had a great time doing the things we've done, from firewood to Fuel Tech. Whatever you choose to do, whether it's an idea outlined in this book or something entirely your own, we know that if you give it your best shot you will come away, as we did, with a sense of fun and accomplishment that is — priceless.